'A comprehensive and clever plan covering all aspects of a vegan diet, with particular focus on effective weight management. There are no gimmicks or fads, instead a combination of the latest research with simple yet delicious recipes that Christine Bailey is rightly known for make *Go Lean Vegan* a must-have diet plan for everyone.'

Ian Marber, Nutritional Therapist and founder of *The Food Doctor*

'Combining cutting up-to-date nutritional research and clinical wisdom on vegan diets, Christine Bailey provides a clear, carefully individualised blueprint for weight loss and good health. *Go Lean Vegan* is, quite simply, the best vegan diet programme book I've seen.'

Dale Pinnock, The Medicinal Chef™

'Christine Bailey's *Go Lean Vegan* is a revolutionary approach to health that fills the gap between a nutritional-based vegan programme and an effective weight loss programme that works. If you are looking to optimise your health, lose weight, boost vitality and follow a delicious plant-based diet this is the book for you. Christine is one of the leading nutritional chefs able to combine science based knowledge into practical and delicious recipes everyone can enjoy.'

Jenny Lee Grace, author of the *Imperfectly Natural* series

'If you want to adopt a vegan way of life, then do it right. *Go Lean Vegan* is a clear, science-based and practical programme that focuses primarily on a healthy vegan diet and is steeped in the nutritional research that underlies all effective weight management'.

Amelia Freer, Nutritional Therapist

About the Author

Christine Bailey, MSc, PGCE mBANT, is an award winning qualified functional nutritionist, chef and food & health consultant. Previously awarded *Coeliac Chef of the Year* she is well known for her inspirational recipes and nutrition expertise. Christine has the ability to merge cutting-edge nutritional science with the practical application required to make healthy eating achievable for everyone.

A member of the Guild of Health Writers, she writes for numerous health, food and fitness magazines and is the author of *The Gut Health Diet, Supercharged Green Juices & Smoothie Diet, Functional Nutrition Cookbook* and *Eat to Get Younger* among others. She has been involved in the health industry for over 18 years and is one of the most respected nutritional experts in the UK focused on evidence based Functional Medicine.

Having transformed her own life and reversed an autoimmune condition in one of her own children Christine now helps to transform the lives of her clients and readers with her science-based approach and practical, no fuss recipes that are accessible for everyone. Christine is sought after both nationally and internationally speaking at numerous health, food and fitness conferences including The Institute of Functional Medicine IFM in the USA.

Go Lean
VEGAN

The Revolutionary
30-day Diet Plan
to Lose Weight and Feel Great

Christine Bailey

yellow
kite

First published in Great Britain in 2016 by Yellow Kite
An imprint of Hodder & Stoughton
An Hachette UK company

First published in paperback in 2017

1

Copyright © Christine Bailey 2016

The right of Christine Bailey to be identified as the Author of the Work has been
asserted by her in accordance with the Copyright, Designs and Patents Act 1988.

A CIP catalogue record for this title is available from the British Library

Paperback ISBN 978 1 473 64208 9
Ebook ISBN 978 1 473 64207 2

Typeset in Sabon MT by Hewer Text UK Ltd, Edinburgh
Printed and bound by Clays Ltd, St Ives plc

The advice here is not intended to replace the services of trained health professionals
or to be a substitute for medical advice. You are advised to consult with your
healthcare professional with regards to matters relating to your health, and in
particular regarding matters that may require diagnosis or medical attention.

Hodder & Stoughton policy is to use papers that are natural, renewable
and recyclable products and made from wood grown in sustainable
forests. The logging and manufacturing processes are expected to
conform to the environmental regulations of the country of origin.

Yellow Kite
Hodder & Stoughton Ltd
Carmelite House
50 Victoria Embankment
London EC4Y 0DZ

www.hodder.co.uk
www.yellowkitebooks.co.uk

Contents

Introduction

Welcome to your fast-track path to a healthy, lean body. The *Go Lean Vegan* diet plan is a revolutionary step-by-step 30-day plan to help you lose weight and start feeling better FAST – while eating delicious, satisfying plant-based foods with absolutely NO calorie counting!

If you're looking to lose weight on a vegan or more plant-based diet but are worried about what to eat and, importantly, how to make it healthy, this programme is for you. Carefully designed, it will get you the results you want and keep you healthy and energised.

The plan works because it addresses the underlying imbalances in the body that can interfere with weight loss and is designed to:

- Cut sugar and reduce grains – preventing insulin from storing more fat in your body
- Tackle cravings and keep you feeling satisfied through the day
- Balance blood sugar and support adrenal function to boost long-lasting energy as you lose weight

···⟩ Support detoxification, digestive health and elimination of toxins for a cleaner, leaner body
···⟩ Boost metabolism and encourage fat burning – giving you real results
···⟩ Lower inflammation – one of the key drivers involved in weight gain, insulin resistance and chronic health conditions
···⟩ Remove common food allergens like gluten and dairy for a long-term health boost

With three meals and optional snacks each day, plus gorgeous but simple recipes to follow on this plan, you won't feel hungry, but full and satisfied. There is no need to count calories – the plan works because it is focused on whole, plant-based foods rich in protein and healthy fats to nourish the body and keep you feeling satisfied.

Whether you are looking to lose a few pounds or seeking a new way of eating to boost your energy levels, *Go Lean Vegan* will provide you with a healthful programme based on scientifically proven nutrition principles for a vibrant, healthy life.

You'll be astounded at how amazing you look and feel in just 30 days.

Why Vegan?

More and more people are discovering the benefits of a vegan or plant-based diet. A vegan diet is one that avoids all animal products including meat, poultry, fish, dairy and eggs. Some people follow a vegan diet for ethical or environmental reasons but over the decades research has also demonstrated the many health benefits, including achieving a healthy, lean body. In fact, studies have found that eating more plant-based protein and fibre can increase fullness, resulting in more effective, long-term weight loss.

In addition to getting you into shape there are many other potential benefits of following a plant-based diet.

Long-term nourishment

The modern Western diet is packed with inflammatory foods, sugar, additives, processed fats, pesticides and hormones, but it is also often lacks in key nutrients, meaning that there is a shortfall in the majority of people's diets. Plants contain nearly all the vital vitamins, minerals, antioxidants, phytonutrients and fibre our bodies need to thrive and, in particular, regulate our metabolism and weight. A nutrient-poor, calorie-rich diet is the major factor behind obesity and diabetes – it's not how much we eat that is important but the quality of the food we eat. By switching to a plant-based diet you can nourish your whole body from within, tackle the underlying imbalances driving poor health and rev up your metabolism. A diet that is abundant in vegetables, beans, pulses, nuts, seeds and fruit will provide you with vital nutrients and more – just a handful of Brazil nuts will supply your daily recommended amount of selenium, while leafy greens, beans and pulses are some of the best food sources of folate, a B vitamin vital for a healthy nervous system and brain. What you choose to put on your fork is more powerful than any pill or medicine when it comes to achieving the body you want and the energy and vitality you long for.

Healthy ageing with plant power antioxidants

Plant-based diets are packed with phytochemicals. These plant compounds are potent antioxidants known for their ability to lower inflammation, protect the body from cell damage and slow down the rate of something called 'telomere shortening', which is linked to ageing. While the structure of your DNA doesn't necessarily alter through your life, what does alter is the extent to which your genes are switched on and off ('expressed'). Epigenetic changes – the food we eat, the environment we live in – can modify the way that our genes function, by not only causing genes that accelerate ageing to be turned on, but by also turning off genes that prevent cancer and other degenerative diseases from taking hold. With the right diet and lifestyle changes, there is the potential to reverse the damaging changes to the way your genes function. Many of the key anti-ageing nutrients are plant chemicals. Nutrients with the most research to date include curcumin (from turmeric), catechins (found in green tea), sulforaphane (from cruciferous vegetables such as broccoli, cabbage and cauliflower) and resveratrol (from the skins of grapes and berries), as well as the B vitamin folate abundant in leafy greens, beans and pulses. A diet packed with these potent plant antioxidants can not only play a key role in how well we age, but has also been associated with lower risk of certain cancers, heart disease and many long-term chronic health conditions.

Blood sugar balance with protein- and fibre-rich plants

Diabetes, insulin resistance and metabolic syndrome are all essentially one problem – poor blood sugar control. Diabetes and associated problems are now considered to be one of the biggest chronic diseases crippling the Western world, particularly the UK and USA. In the UK alone it is estimated that 4 million people are living with diabetes, about 6 per cent of the population (1 in every 16 people). This is expected to rise to 5 million by 2025. People with diabetes are four times more likely to die from heart disease and have a four-fold increased risk of dementia. Yet research has shown us that diabetes is reversible, especially if caught in the early stages. For example, one study showed that even people with advanced type-2 diabetes (where the pancreatic insulin-producing cells have been damaged) can recover and diabetes reversed in just one week through dramatic changes in diet. The quality of the food (rather than calories in/calories out) has been shown to be more powerful in balancing blood sugar and driving our metabolism and health. A diet based on whole foods that are unprocessed and rich in fibre is particularly important for improving blood sugar balance. Fibre is important because it slows the absorption of sugar from the gut into the bloodstream, makes us feel full and lowers cholesterol. Studies have shown that adding fibre to the diet can be as effective as diabetes medication in lowering blood sugar. Other studies of people with type 2 diabetes found that simply replacing two servings of red meat with legumes three times a week improved cholesterol and blood sugar. Switching to a plant-based diet will not only balance your blood sugar levels but will help you feel more satisfied after meals, meaning you'll find it easier to lose weight and maintain a healthy weight without feeling deprived or hungry.

Diets rich in fibre have numerous other health benefits, associated with lowering risks of certain cancers and also heart disease. Fibre is also essential for maintaining a healthy digestive system and in particular supporting a healthy gut flora. Often known as probiotics, these beneficial microbes are known to play a vital role in many body systems, including supporting our immune system, detoxifying hormones, boosting our mood and even helping to keep us slim. Fibre is also important for detoxification and the elimination of waste from the body.

Keeping your heart healthy

Whether you are overweight or not, as we age our risk of cardio-vascular disease increases. And if you are carrying excess weight, particularly around the belly, then your risk of heart disease is greater. Whether you are concerned about high blood pressure, raised triglycerides and cholesterol or just want to optimise your heart health a plant-based diet can help. Plant foods are rich in protective antioxidants to help lower inflammation and reduce the risk of damage to the arteries. They are also packed with key heart-healthy nutrients such as potassium, magnesium and B vitamins (particularly folate) and, of course, plenty of fibre to maintain healthy cholesterol levels. Certain studies have found diets rich in plant foods tend to result in lower body weight, lower cholesterol and lower blood pressure levels.

Fighting inflammation

Chronic low-level inflammation is now known to be a key driver in many age-related, degenerative diseases, including heart disease, obesity, diabetes, cancer, dementia and depression. In fact, inflammation actually causes insulin resistance, further promoting more inflammation in the body and making it harder for you to lose weight. If you are carrying excess weight especially around the tummy area, it is likely you are already suffering with low-grade inflammation – the trouble is it's invisible and doesn't hurt in the same way that a sports injury would. One of the key drivers of this inflammation is the diet we eat. Sugar, refined carbohydrates, damaged fats, excess animal protein (particularly processed meats), processed oils, artificial sweeteners, food allergies and intolerances, stress and a sedentary lifestyle can all promote inflammation. The *Go Lean Vegan* diet tackles these underlying triggers to deal with inflammation at the root cause. In addition, a plant-based diet contains numerous natural anti-inflammatory compounds to further lower inflammation. For example, turmeric contains curcumin, known for its ability to lower inflammation throughout the body and reduce the risk of conditions such as Alzheimer's, inflammatory bowel disease, allergies, asthma, arthritis and diabetes – to name a few. Other foods like pineapple and papaya contain the digestive enzymes bromelain and papain, known to lower inflammation and improve recovery after exercise or injuries. Flaxseed, hemp, chia seeds and leafy greens all contain anti-inflammatory Omega-3 fats, while avocados and olive oil are good sources of monounsaturated fats, which have anti-inflammatory benefits.

Go Lean Vegan – Your Fast Track to Weight Loss

Go Lean Vegan works because it addresses underlying imbalances in the body that can contribute to weight gain. Some vegan diets fail because they are low in protein (needed to balance blood sugar and tackle cravings), fibre (key when it comes to stopping you feeling hungry), healthy fats (essential for improved cell function and a healthy metabolism) or key vitamins and minerals. Go Lean Vegan is different. The programme has been carefully designed to ensure successful weight loss while providing the body with all the essential nutrients it needs for a healthy body long term.

Here are just some of the reasons why Go Lean Vegan works:

A focus on real foods

Not all vegan diets are healthy. Skip the processed fake foods, ready meals, refined products and junk food and simply focus on real, whole plant foods, which are packed with the nutrients your body needs. And that doesn't mean you have to spend hours in the kitchen – the recipes are quick and easy to prepare and cook and taste delicious.

Ensures protein power

Consuming enough protein is essential for effective weight loss. Many vegan diets are simply far too low in protein. Studies have consistently shown protein increases fat burning and helps curb the appetite, keeping you feeling fuller for longer. Following a vegan diet can make it harder to consume the right levels of protein for weight loss. It also needs to be varied to ensure you get all the essential amino acids your body needs to function optimally. For this reason, I've included a wide range of protein-rich foods plus vegan protein powders to ensure you not only lose weight fast but develop a lean, strong healthy body (see pages 14–19 for more on protein).

Slow carbs not no carbs

Many vegan and vegetarian diets fail because they are heavily centred on eating starchy carbs – whether bowls of pasta and rice, breads, crackers or cookies. The trouble is that these refined carbohydrates have a devastating effect on your blood sugar levels, leading to big spikes in sugar and insulin. In increased levels insulin tells your body to store fat, particularly around your tummy and also drives inflammation and oxidative damage to the body. In the long term it will increase your risk of insulin resistance, making it harder for you to lose weight. So this plan eliminates refined sugar and starches and instead focuses on slower-releasing carbohydrates.

A true plant-based diet is naturally lower in carbohydrates as it is based around colourful vegetables. When you focus on plants you are actually filling up with low-glycemic (slow-releasing) fibre-rich foods that will have little impact on your blood sugar, making it easier for you to lose weight. The *Go Lean Vegan* plan therefore encourages you to eat plenty of salads, stews, casseroles and soups flavoured with spices and herbs to create nourishing and satisfying meals.

Supports detoxification

Our bodies are exposed to a number of environmental toxins – from the food we eat, the air we breathe and the water we drink, as well as the countless toxins in our homes and surroundings. It is now accepted that environmental toxins are linked to many chronic health conditions, but did you also know that toxins can make you fat? Many environmental chemicals can disrupt blood sugar balance, promote inflammation and may even be linked to diabetes. Supporting your body's detoxification system is crucial if you want to optimise your health and achieve long-term weight loss. There are several ways in which a plant-based vegan diet supports detoxification. Firstly, it is packed with natural foods rich in water, which hydrates the body and contributes to our fluid intake, supporting elimination. It is also packed with fibre meaning regular bowel movements that help to excrete toxins. But many plant-based foods also contain key compounds that enhance our natural detoxification pathways. For example, cruciferous vegetables like broccoli, cauliflower, kale and watercress contain special phytochemicals called glucosinolates, which support liver function. Other notable detox-friendly foods include berries, pomegranate, turmeric, onion, garlic, green tea, citrus, beetroot and many herbs. Eating a plant-based diet also excludes many toxins present in meat, fish and dairy products.

Includes healthy fats

Forget low-fat diets – not only do they not work but they are actually damaging to your health. Your body and brain (in fact, all your cells) need fat. Fat is also very satisfying and does not disrupt blood sugar making it ideal for helping you lose weight. The right fats can also improve blood sugar balance, lower inflammation and improve insulin function. But watch the type of fats you consume – don't eat soybean oil, sunflower oil or corn oil as these are heavily processed, refined, high in Omega-6 and easily oxidised. These are not beneficial to your health and are likely to promote inflammation. The *Go Lean Vegan* plan encourages you to eat the right types of healthy fats, including extra-virgin olive oil, coconut, avocado and macadamia nut oils and seed oils like flaxseed and chia seed, as well as plant foods like olives, avocadoes, nuts and seeds, coconut and even leafy greens.

Removes common food allergens

Can't lose weight? It may be linked to an underlying food sensitivity or allergy. Many people are familiar with the idea of acute allergies, where eating a peanut, for example, causes sudden reactions that cause the sufferer to break out in hives or their throat to swell. Food sensitivities might not be as dramatic but can lead to ongoing inflammation that may disrupt blood sugar levels, contributing to weight gain and making it harder to lose weight. Various studies have shown that eliminating common food reactions like gluten and dairy can help improve blood sugar balance and weight loss. Although a vegan diet is naturally dairy-free it can often be high in gluten grains. The *Go Lean Vegan* diet eliminates all gluten to help lower inflammation, support digestion and improve your ability to lose weight.

Gluten is found in wheat, barley and rye and numerous products containing these grains. It's a hot topic these days – there are now hundreds of gluten-free products on the shelves, but many of these are highly processed, refined and laden with sugar. The response to gluten is complex. You don't have to be coeliac (an autoimmune condition triggered by gluten) to have a problem with gluten; it can provoke low-grade inflammation in almost anyone and has been linked to a diverse range of conditions from depression, IBS, migraines and autoimmune conditions to weight gain. It can damage the gut lining, allowing bugs and partially digested food proteins to enter your bloodstream and provoke an immune reaction. It is now clear from the research that gluten sensitivity is much more common than coeliac disease and may be a contributing factor affecting your health.

In addition to removing gluten from your diet the *Go Lean Vegan* plan avoids an over reliance on the grains typically found in many vegan or vegetarian diets. This keeps the carbohydrate intake down. This doesn't mean you won't be eating any carbs – the plan includes plenty of carbs from beans and pulses, sweet potato and some pseudo grains like quinoa, buckwheat and millet as well as fruits and vegetables. These have the added bonus of being rich in essential minerals, protein, fibre and vitamins to keep you nourished and energised.

Recommends fermented foods

Optimising health and improving weight loss relies on a healthy digestive tract. The bugs in your gut not only control digestion, metabolism and inflammation, but new research is demonstrating how they can also affect your weight. Certain bacteria appear to encourage fat burning while others increase body fat and insulin resistance. Gut bacteria thrive on what you feed them – including plenty of plant foods rich in fermentable fibre which encourages beneficial bacteria to grow. But you can also improve your gut flora by consuming fermented foods like coconut yoghurt, coconut kefir, miso, tempeh, natto, sauerkraut and kimchi.

They are naturally rich in beneficial microbes (often referred to as probiotics) known to support digestion, and are also easier to digest and absorb making them particularly nutritious. By including fermented foods in your diet you naturally improve digestive health and benefit from the more bioavailable nutrients they contain.

Follows a vegan paleo approach

Obviously the plan doesn't include meat, but paleo and vegan diets are alike when it comes to avoiding processed foods and sticking to real whole foods for optimal nutrition. One of the reasons why a paleo diet can help with weight loss is that it eliminates carbohydrate-rich grains and focuses more on antioxidant-rich vegetables and healthy fats from nuts, seeds and foods like avocado. It also avoids key allergen foods and foods known to promote inflammation and irritate the gut such as eggs, dairy and gluten grains. The *Go Lean Vegan* plan does include a few pseudo grains like buckwheat, teff and quinoa as these are useful protein foods for vegans. However, there is a greater emphasis on carbohydrates from beans, pulses and vegetables with limited fruits.

Keeping It Healthy

The *Go Lean Vegan* plan is not a fad diet but one that is focused on nutrient dense and varied plant foods to provide all the essential nutrients you need to thrive while losing weight. The following gives you all the information you need on what those nutrients are and how to include them in your diet.

Protein: How to Get Enough

One of the biggest concerns with following a vegan diet is obtaining sufficient protein. This is particularly important for weight loss as it helps support muscle mass, metabolism, balances blood sugar and keeps you feeling fuller through the day.

Protein is an important building block for bones, muscles, cartilage and skin and provides the essential amino acids the body needs for repairing tissues and producing hormones and enzymes. In total, there are around 20 amino acids that the human body uses to build proteins, classified as either essential or non-essential. Your body can produce non-essential amino acids but it cannot produce those essential amino acids we need, which have to be obtained through your diet. Animal protein sources, such as meat, fish, poultry, eggs and dairy are considered to be complete sources of protein because they contain all of the essential amino acids that your body needs to function effectively. In contrast, most plant protein sources, such as beans, lentils, nuts and seeds are considered to be incomplete, as they lack one or more of the essential amino acids. There are only a few plant foods considered complete proteins – these include soy, spirulina, quinoa and amaranth – even more reason to consume a variety of plant foods daily.

For effective weight loss consuming a sufficient amount of protein daily is key. The recommended dietary allowance (RDA) is around 0.8g per kg of body weight. So for a 64-kg (10-stone) woman this would be around 51g of protein. This is easily achievable on a vegan diet. However, a growing body of research indicates that this amount is inadequate. In fact our protein intake should be well above the current RDA to support weight loss, blood sugar balance, appetite regulation and healthy ageing. Higher protein diets also improve feelings of fullness and lead to greater reductions in body weight and fat mass compared with standard protein diets. Current evidence indicates that a protein intake of 1.2–1.6g (per kg body weight) is a more ideal target. This is particularly relevant to anyone following a vegan diet because plant proteins are not digested as well as animal proteins. So to support weight loss and a healthy lean body aim for at least 1.2g per kg daily – about 68g protein a day if you are a woman weighing 64kg (10 stone). To put this in to context, you will need to consume at least 20g of protein at each meal, plus additional if you are including a snack. As essential amino acids are so important for muscle mass and a lean body composition, many vegans will benefit from taking a branched chain amino acid formula (BCAA). For information on supplements see page 38.

Cooking foods improves protein digestibility so it is recommended you include a variety of cooked and raw foods daily. Aim for a range of protein sources such as soy products (see pages 40–42), cooked beans and lentils, sprouted beans, nuts and seeds and leafy greens and consider the use of protein powders. The table on page 17 highlights some of the top protein plant-based foods to consume – you will need to include around 3–4 servings of these foods each day. Aim for around 20g protein at each meal and if you do snack, make sure to include protein. Many protein powders contain around 20–30g protein per serving and make it easier to ensure you meet your daily needs. If you are struggling with blood sugar imbalances or diabetes, consider taking amino acid formulas or branched chain amino acid formulas as you transition into a vegan style of eating to make sure you getting all the essential amino acids you need.

Here are some ideas on how to boost your protein intake:

···→ If using a milk alternative and not making your own (see page 79) try hemp, coconut or soya milk rather than almond or rice milk as these tend to be higher in protein
···→ Nuts and seeds make a useful snack – try and include shelled hemp seeds as these are higher in protein than other seeds
···→ If your lunch or breakfast is a little lower in protein make up for it with a higher protein snack (Grab-and-Go Vanilla and Chocolate Chip Protein Bars, page 105 or Superberry Protein Balls, page 274) or swap a snack with a protein smoothie
···→ Remember that leafy greens like kale and spinach and cruciferous vegetables like broccoli and cauliflower are

good sources of protein – aim for 1–2 cups daily with your meals

---> Teff flour is particularly rich in protein so try the Teff Chocolate Bread (page 284) as a healthy way to boost your protein intake

---> Spirulina is high in protein so add a spoonful to a smoothie or blend into one of the salad dressings or sauces

---> Check food packaging labels – the protein content of different brands of tofu, for example, can vary widely

---> When making any soup consider adding or blending in tins of cooked beans, nut butter or silken tofu to naturally boost protein content

---> Quinoa is higher in protein than brown rice so choose this where possible. It is also richer in valuable minerals like magnesium

---> Bags of frozen peas and shelled edamame (soybeans) are convenient sources of protein

Protein Content of Foods in *Go Lean Vegan* (note protein content may vary between different brands)

Food	Protein (grams)
Soy products	
Tempeh (166g/1 cup)..31g	
Tofu, firm (126g/½ cup)..10g	
Tofu, silken (100g) 5g	
Legumes	
Black beans, cooked (172g/1 cup) 15g	

Kidney beans, cooked (176g/1 cup)..................................16g

Lentils, cooked (198g/1 cup).......................................18g

Cannellini beans, cooked (179g/1 cup) 17g

Butter beans, cooked (188g/1 cup)...............................15g

Chickpeas, cooked (164g/1 cup) 15g

Milk alternatives

Almond milk (240ml/1 cup) 1g

Hemp milk (240ml/1 cup) 5g

Coconut milk (240ml/1 cup).......................................5g

Soya milk (240ml/1 cup) 8g

Nuts and seeds

Almonds (28g)...6g

Chia (28g) 4g

Hemp (28g)..10g

Flaxseed (28g) 5g

Cashews (28g) 5g

Pecans (28g) 3g

Peanuts (28g)..8g

Peanut butter (2 tbsp)...8g

Almond nut butter (2 tbsp) 4g

Tahini paste (2 tbsp)..6g

Pumpkin seeds (28g) 5g

Sunflower seeds (28g) 6g

Brazil nuts (28g)...4g

Vegetables

Broccoli (½ cup cooked or 1 cup raw)..............................2g

Cauliflower (½ cup cooked or 1 cup raw) 1g

Peas, frozen (½ cup cooked or 1 cup raw) 4.5g

Spinach (½ cup cooked or 1 cup raw) 2.5g

Kale (½ cup cooked or 1 cup raw) 1g

Mushrooms (½ cup cooked or 1 cup raw).......................1.5g

Green beans (½ cup cooked or 1 cup raw).........................1g

Sweet potato (1 medium)..2g

Sweetcorn, tinned (½ cup cooked or 1 cup raw)...............2g

Pseudo grains

Quinoa, cooked (½ cup)...4g

Buckwheat, cooked (½ cup) 3g

Millet, cooked (½ cup)...3g

Oats, cooked (½ cup) 3g

Brown rice, cooked (½ cup) 2.5g

Amaranth, cooked (½ cup)...4.5g

Teff flour (80g/½ cup)..10g

Protein powders and superfoods

Spirulina (1 tbsp) 4g

Vegan protein powder (20–30g/1 scoop) 20g–30g

Nori sheets (28g)..2g

Ditch the Weight with Healthy Fats

Many people are still fearful of fat, thinking that it will cause them to put on weight. Nothing could be more wrong. While fat may be higher in calories than protein or carbohydrates, eating fat does not have the same impact on your weight or metabolism. In fact, as I've explained earlier, eating the right types of fat can actually boost weight loss and metabolism. Not only that, eating more fat shuts off your brain's hunger and craving centres, keeping you satisfied for longer.

The *Go Lean Vegan* plan incorporates a range of healthy quality fats in the diet to boost weight loss and improve overall health. By including these fats in a plant-based diet that's low in refined carbohydrates, low-glycemic and high in fibre, you will get the results you want without feeling deprived.

The healthy fats to include are the Omega-3 and Omega-6 polyunsaturated fats (PUFAs), and Omega-9 monounsaturated fats (MUFAs). Good plant sources include avocados, coconut oil, olive oil, olives, nuts and seeds. Including fat with each meal can also help with the absorption of fat-soluble vitamins. For example, carotenoid-rich foods like carrots or tomatoes, which provide the precursor to vitamin A, are more easily absorbed with cooking and the addition of fat.

Omega-3 – are you getting enough?

One of the types of fats vegans can be low in are the essential anti-inflammatory Omega-3 fats known as alpha-linolenic acid (ALA) and its derivatives EPA and DHA. ALA is a short-chain Omega-3 fatty acid found in flaxseed, chia seeds, walnuts, hemp and some soy products, as well as oily fish. But it is actually EPA and DHA that are the most beneficial to health and healthy ageing and have powerful anti-inflammatory effects. These fats also increase levels of the hormone adiponectin, which helps to prevent insulin resistance making it easier to lose weight. They have also been shown to boost metabolism too. Unfortunately, EPA and DHA are predominately present in animal foods such as oily fish. While we can convert ALA from plant foods into these active Omega-3 fats the conversion is poor. This means vegans are often low in both DHA and EPA even if they are eating lots of ALA-rich foods like flaxseed.

A second type of essential fatty acid is linoleic acid (LA), an Omega-6 fat. However, this is readily abundant in plant foods and present in many nuts, seeds and vegetable oils. In fact, most people get far too much Omega-6 fat in their diet. Not only does this cause an imbalance between levels of Omega-6 and Omega-3 fats, which promotes inflammation but a high intake of Omega-6 actually reduces the conversion of Omega-3 fats into valuable DHA and EPA. The ideal ratio of Omega-6 to Omega-3 is around 3:1 yet most of us have ratios up to 20:1. Vegans are more prone to this imbalance as Omega-3 intake is often low. To address this imbalance focus more on Omega-3-rich foods (flaxseed, chia seeds, walnuts, pumpkin seeds) and avoid vegetable oils to reduce your Omega-6 intake. You may also benefit from a DHA supplement, which can be derived from algae sources rather than fish.

Another group of fats important for health are monounsaturated fats or Omega-9 fats. Known for their anti-inflammatory properties these are found in plant foods such as olives, macadamia nuts and avocados.

While a vegan diet is naturally low in saturated fat, contrary to popular (but misguided) belief, there is a place for a small amount of saturated fat in the diet. Coconut oil is an example of a plant saturated fat and is particularly beneficial because it is very heat-stable, making it one of the best oils to cook with. Coconut oil is rich in medium-chain triglycerides (MCTs), which are less likely than animal fats to be stored in your fat cells and more likely to be burned for energy. Moreover, using MCTs as the main type of saturated fat in your diet may reduce your overall food intake and promote weight loss.

Here are some tips on the best sources of healthy fats and how to include them in your diet:

⟶ Nuts and seeds are not only rich in healthy fats but are packed with key vitamins and minerals, protein and fibre. Enjoy a variety such as macadamia, almond, peanut, cashew, pistachio, pecan and Brazil nuts and flaxseed, sunflower, sesame, hemp, chia and pumpkin seeds. Aim to include 2 tablespoons of Omega-3 rich nuts and seeds (or nut and seed butters) daily

⟶ Include 1–2 cups of leafy green vegetables a day as they can also provide Omega-3 fats

⟶ Soy products also contain Omega-3 so include these 1–2 times a week, if possible

⟶ Include daily foods rich in monounsaturated fats – this includes olives, olive oil, avocados and macadamia nuts

⟶ Include coconut milk, coconut yoghurt and kefir in your diet for additional MCT fats

⟶ Oils – opt for organic cold-pressed virgin oils where possible such as coconut, avocado, nut and seed oils and olive oil (use normal olive oil to cook with and extra-virgin olive oil for salads and dressings). Omega-3 rich nut and seed oils such as flaxseed and walnut are vulnerable to heat so are best used in dressings, dips or smoothies. You can also drizzle them over soups and steamed vegetables. Coconut oil is one of the best oils for cooking as it is less chemically altered by heat than other oils. Avoid sunflower, soy, corn and vegetable oils and heated and processed refined oils and spreads, including sunflower margarines. Avoid any foods with the word 'hydrogenated' on the label

⟶ Consider taking an algae supplement of DHA

Getting Your Carbs Right

The low-carb frenzy has ebbed and flowed in popularity and many people achieve great results by cutting the carbs. A very low-carb diet is difficult for vegans since the majority of plant foods fall into the carbs category, particularly useful high protein foods such as beans and pulses. But there is a great different between the impact of different types of carbs. Vegetables, beans, pulses and some fruits are referred to as slow carbs, which are low-glycaemic and don't spike your blood sugar or insulin. The lower the glycaemic load of the food you consume the slower it will raise your blood sugar and the easier you will find it to lose weight. By contrast, high-glycaemic foods such as refined and processed foods, grains, cakes, biscuits, breads and pasta as well as fizzy drinks, dried fruit and fruit juices will trigger soaring blood sugar spikes and raised insulin. This will encourage your body to dump excess glucose as fat on your body and result in energy dips followed by cravings for more sugary foods to pick you up – and so the see-saw effect continues. This ultimately leads to weight gain, blood sugar imbalances and the road to diabetes.

The added benefit of slow carbs is that they come loaded with nutrients, fibre and protective antioxidants called phytochemicals. So not only are they nutrient-rich but they are one of the best groups of foods to include for weight loss and long-term health. High-fibre, low-glycaemic carbs, such as leafy green vegetables and many other vegetables, are slowly digested and don't lead to blood sugar and insulin spikes; they will also protect, nourish and energise the body.

PILE YOUR PLATE

At least half of your plate should be filled with a colourful selection of these vegetables: asparagus, aubergine, beansprouts, beet greens, broccoli, Brussels sprouts, cabbage, cauliflower, celery, chives, collard greens, courgettes, cucumber, dandelion greens, endive, fennel, garlic, ginger (fresh), globe artichoke, green beans, jalapeño peppers, kale, lettuces (all types), mushrooms, mustard greens, onions (all types), pak choi, palm hearts, parsley, peppers (all colours), radicchio, radishes, rocket, shallots, spinach, spring greens, Swiss chard, tomatoes, turnip greens, watercress.

EAT PLENTY

These fibre- and protein-rich foods contain slow-release carbohydrates so will prevent insulin spikes and keep you feeling fuller for longer. Aim for 3–4 portions daily and include a wide variety: butter beans, black beans, cannellini beans, chickpeas, edamame (soybeans), kidney beans, lentils, pinto beans, split peas. A serving is around 3/4 cup (around 130g) cooked weight.

EAT IN MODERATION

Delicious gluten-free grains (many of which provide a source of protein) and starchy vegetables are included in this category – aim for one portion daily and ideally eat these with your evening meal: amaranth, buckwheat, gluten-free oats, millet, quinoa, rice (brown, black and red) and beetroot, carrots, sweet potato. A serving of grains is 1/3 cup (40–60g) cooked grains or ½ cup (around 100g) cooked starchy vegetables (e.g. carrots, sweet potato, butternut squash).

Dark berries (blueberries, cherries, raspberries, blackberries etc.) and citrus fruits are filled with phytonutrients, known for their health-boosting benefits. They are also the best low-glycaemic fruits to consume. Stone fruits like nectarines, plums, apples and pears are also slow releasing and a good source of fibre. In total include 1–2 portions of fruit daily, focusing on these low-glycaemic fruits.

EAT IN LIMITED AMOUNTS

Watch your intake of high-sugar fruits – these include tropical fruits like melons, grapes and pineapple so include these occasionally and always combine with some protein and/or fat. Dried fruit is high in sugar and should be generally avoided, although it is very occasionally used in a couple of recipes when combined with protein to help slow down the release of sugars.

AVOID COMPLETELY

Gluten-containing whole grains are common allergens and can promote inflammation in the body, making it harder to lose weight. Steer clear of wheat, barley, rye, spelt and products containing them. Processed foods such as pasta, bread, low-fat sweetened products and processed vegan foods should likewise be avoided, as well as all sugars and artificial sweeteners, including agave nectar, organic cane juice, cane syrup, maple syrup, molasses, etc.

On the *Go Lean Vegan* programme, about 75 per cent of your carb intake should come from non-starchy vegetables plus a little low-glycaemic fruit. You should be piling vegetables on your plate at every meal – this will not only nourish your body but will fill you up, making it easier to shift excess weight.

Which carbs, when and how much should I eat?

Slow-burning, low-glycaemic vegetables should form the basis of your diet during the 30-day programme. However, it's important to bear in mind that not all carbs are equal, so some carbs should be eaten in moderation or limited amounts. And, of course, highly processed foods should be avoided completely.

In addition, studies indicate that if you want to improve your metabolism, quality of sleep, cognitive function and energy during the day then the timing of carbohydrate consumption is important. Essentially it is better to limit carbohydrate consumption at breakfast and lunch and eat more starchy vegetables or gluten-free grain with the evening meal.

Cutting Back the Sugar

Go Lean Vegan works because it focuses on real foods and, in particular, restricts your intake of sugar. If you want to lose weight and get healthy you need to ditch the sugar. And that means avoiding processed foods: hidden sugars lurk in even so-called 'healthy' foods so always read the ingredients labels – even for foods that don't taste sweet.

That doesn't mean you can't enjoy the odd sweet treat but aim to get it from the natural sweetness found in fruits and other foods, without resorting to the sugar overload of processed foods. There are a number of recipes for 'feel-good' treats, which are naturally sweetened with fruits or a little xylitol or stevia, both sugar substitutes that are unlikely to disrupt blood sugar levels. Read labels carefully: some stevia is actually blended with cane sugar making it no better for you than regular sugar. Choose a granulated stevia with erythritol or xylitol added or a pure liquid stevia.

SHOULD YOU SNACK?

You may have heard that snacking throughout the day can keep your metabolism up. However, this is a myth. Studies in people who consumed the same number of calories in seven meals as opposed to two meals found no difference in calories burned between the two groups. One of the dangers with constant snacking is over-consuming food, as well as placing additional pressure on the digestive system. Ideally try not to snack in between meals. However if you find yourself going long periods without food and your blood sugar is dipping too much then you may need to include a healthy snack initially while your body adapts (see pages 237–261). For some people with fatigue, poor adrenal health or blood sugar imbalances, including a snack could be helpful – just make sure it contains plenty of protein and/or some healthy fats to avoid sudden changes in blood sugar levels. However the ideal is that you move to eating just three protein-rich meals a day.

Managing cravings

Changing your diet can be tough, especially if you have a sweet tooth. Balancing your blood sugar throughout the day is the best way to manage cravings. The best way to do this is to ditch the processed sugary foods and artificial sweeteners and combine protein, good fats and healthy carbs with each meal. The same is true when you reach for a snack – an apple with a handful of nuts is better than a piece of fruit on its own.

If you do suffer from cravings here are a few tips:

···› Have a protein-rich breakfast – not only will it help you lose weight but it is likely to reduce cravings throughout the day. The breakfast options in this plan are designed to contain sufficient protein to energise you and keep blood sugar balanced. Make use of the protein powders to boast your morning protein intake – aim for 20g

···› Consider taking branched chain amino acids (BCAA) initially to stimulate lean muscle and balance blood sugar

···› Avoid drinking your sugar and calories – alcohol, fizzy drinks, fruit juices and squash not only drive up your appetite and waist size but are a sure way to trigger more cravings

···› If you do need a snack, particularly in the afternoon when you might be having a blood sugar dip, go for a protein- and fibre-rich option (nuts, seeds and beans are ideal)

···› Skip the caffeine. Coffee is more likely to lead to cravings as caffeine can disrupt blood sugar levels. Caffeine can also disrupt your circadian rhythm, which can disrupt sleep and in turn increase cravings for sugary foods. Switch to herbal teas, water, dandelion coffee or a little green tea, which contains only a little caffeine and has been shown to help with fat burning. If you drink a lot of caffeine then start cutting it out gradually before starting the programme

⋯⟩ Take steps to address any ongoing stress and include daily exercise and time for relaxation. Stress hormones like cortisol can activate cravings and disrupt our blood sugar levels. When you are stressed it is also more diffi-cult to be mindful about what you are eating

⋯⟩ Take a walk. If a craving strikes get moving. Exercise will not only boost your mood but will distract your mind away from the food you are craving. Exercise will also rev up your metabolism helping you to burn more fat

⋯⟩ Get plenty of sleep. Lack of sleep has been associated with weight gain, insulin resistance and drives sugar cravings by affecting your hunger hormones

Essential Minerals and Vitamins

One of the concerns that many people have when considering a vegan diet is whether they will get enough of the essential vita-mins and minerals they need, particularly calcium and iron.

Calcium

Calcium is one of the most important minerals in the body and is particularly important for women as it can help prevent osteopor-osis. Many people worry that a dairy-free diet will not provide sufficient calcium, but if you focus on real, plant foods there is no reason why it should not supply optimal amounts.

A key point to consider is how much calcium you *absorb*, rather than how much you actually *consume*. People generally absorb about 25–30 per cent of the calcium in their diets although absorption rates can vary. Calcium absorption from cow's milk is about 30 per cent; absorption rates are about the same for calcium-set tofu and for many fortified plant milks. Absorption rates for other plant foods vary from as little as 5 per cent to as much as 65 per cent. Therefore, the focus is on consuming foods that are not only good sources of calcium, but good sources of well-absorbed calcium. For example, while leafy greens are often rich in calcium, some of them are also high in oxalates, compounds that bind calcium and reduce its absorption. High-oxalate vegetables include spinach, beet greens and chard so are not considered good sources of calcium. On the other hand kale, mustard greens, turnip greens and broccoli are low in oxalates so we absorb calcium from these foods well. In addition, many of these foods also contain other important nutrients for bone health such as magnesium, potassium, vitamin C and vitamin K.

Beans, nuts and seeds provide moderate amounts of calcium but do not appear to be absorbed very efficiently, although soaking nuts and seeds (see page 79) can improve absorption. Calcium absorption from edamame (soybeans) seems to be higher than from other beans. Tofu is often prepared using calcium sulphate making it a particularly rich source of calcium. In addition, many of the milk alternatives are fortified with calcium and vitamin D, making them useful ways to increase your intake.

The daily recommended amount of calcium for women following a vegan diet is 1000mg, based on the assumption that most people absorb around 30 per cent of it. To help meet your calcium needs you will need around 6 servings of calcium-rich foods daily.

Calcium-rich Foods

Beans and pulses
Black beans, cooked (½ cup) 51mg
Chickpeas, cooked (½ cup) 40mg
Kidney beans, cooked (½ cup)..25mg
Lentils, cooked (½ cup) 19mg

Soy products
Tofu (processed with calcium sulphate) (½ cup).............150–300mg
Silken tofu (½ cup) 30mg
Fortified soy milk (240ml/1 cup).......................................250–300mg
Edamame (soybeans) (½ cup)..87mg
Tempeh (83g/½ cup)..92mg

Nuts and seeds
Sesame seeds (2 tbsp)..140mg
Tahini paste (2 tbsp)..128mg
Almond nut butter (2 tbsp) 111mg
Almonds (30g)...94mg
Chia seeds (30g)..177mg
Hemp seeds (30g)..57mg
Almond milk, fortified (240ml/1 cup)......................................450mg

Vegetables
Pak choi, cooked (½ cup) 79mg
Kale, cooked (½ cup) 90mg
Broccoli, cooked (½ cup)..43mg
Collard greens, cooked (½ cup) 133mg
Sweet potato, cooked (½ cup)..45mg

Turnip greens, cooked (½ cup) 98mg
Okra, cooked (½ cup) 68mg

Fruits
Dried figs (½ cup)..120mg
Raisins (½ cup)...41mg
Orange juice, fortified (240ml/1cup) 300mg

Vitamin D

Adequate vitamin D is just as important for bone health as calcium. Current research has also revealed that suboptimal vitamin D levels are also linked to numerous health conditions, including heart disease, diabetes, depression, autoimmune conditions and cancer. The main source of vitamin D is actually sunlight – we can make vitamin D by exposure of our skin to the sun. Therefore try and expose your skin to sunlight for 15–30 minutes each day. Food sources of vitamin D are very limited, the main sources being oily fish, eggs and offal. For vegans food sources include vitamin D-fortified foods like milk alternatives and mushrooms. Many people are therefore likely to benefit from supplementation.

Remember of course that one of the best ways to look after your bones in the long term is to stay physically active. Choose weight-bearing and high-impact exercise – aim for at least half an hour a day of brisk walking, weight lifting, aerobics, dancing, jogging or rebounding (trampolining), or sports such as football, tennis or squash.

Iron and zinc

Two other minerals that can be low in vegan diets are iron and zinc. Unfortunately both are absorbed less well from plant foods than from animal products. This is partly due to the presence of phytates in certain foods, which bind to minerals making them less absorbable. As a key component of red blood cells, iron is essential in the transport of oxygen throughout the body. Low levels can therefore lead to fatigue and poor cognitive function. Because iron from plant-based foods isn't absorbed as easily as iron from meat, vegans are often recommended to consume almost twice as much iron as meat eaters. However, by including vitamin C-rich foods with each meal you can improve absorption. The daily recommended amount for women is 14.8mg.

There are a number of ways you can naturally increase your body's absorption of iron and zinc

- Fermented foods increase mineral availability so include these if possible
- Add vitamin C-rich vegetables and fruits (citrus fruits, red peppers, leafy greens, broccoli, cauliflower, berries) at every meal to enhance absorption of iron
- Cook in an iron pan, especially when you are cooking with more acidic foods like tomatoes as this can improve your iron intake
- Soaking and toasting nuts and seeds, beans and grains can reduce the effects of phytates, aiding absorption of minerals
- Sprouting beans and grains can also improve absorption (see page 40)
- Avoid taking calcium and iron supplements together as they can interfere with absorption
- Avoid drinking coffee and tea with meals to maximise iron absorption

···> Include iron-rich foods daily such as leafy greens, sea vegetables (dulse, nori, wakame), prunes, lentils, beans, edamame (soybeans), cashew nuts, dark chocolate, almonds

···> Include zinc-rich foods daily such as tahini paste, dark chocolate, edamame (soybeans), tempeh, tofu, pumpkin seeds, cashew nuts, sunflower seeds, Brazil nuts, tinned beans, mushrooms, quinoa, millet

Iron-rich Foods

Beans and pulses

Edamame (soybeans), cooked (½ cup) 4.4g

Lentils, cooked (½ cup) 3.3g

Black beans, cooked (½ cup) 1.8g

Kidney beans, cooked (½ cup)..2g

Split peas, cooked (½ cup)...1.3g

Chickpeas , cooked (½ cup)..2.4g

Cannellini beans, cooked (½ cup) 2.2g

Soy products

Tofu, cooked (½ cup) 2g

Tempeh, cooked (½ cup)...1.3g

Vegetables

Spinach, cooked (½ cup)...3.2g

Beet greens, cooked (½ cup)..1.4g

Asparagus, cooked (½ cup) 0.8g

Pak choi, cooked (½ cup) 0.9g

Collard greens, cooked (½ cup) 1.1g

Peas, cooked (½ cup) 1.2g

Pumpkin, cooked (½ cup)...1.7g

Dulse, dry (½ cup) 11.2g

Grains

Quinoa, cooked (½ cup)..1.4g

Brown rice, cooked (½ cup) 0.4g

Nuts and seeds

Cashews (¼ cup) 2g

Peanuts (¼ cup)..1.7g

Tahini paste (2 tbsp)..2.7g

Almonds (¼ cup)..1.3g

Chocolate

Dark chocolate (30g) 3.9g

B12: the missing vitamin

If you are following a vegan diet you will need to take a vitamin
B12 supplement or consume B12-fortified foods like nutritional
yeast flakes. Vitamin B12 is needed for cell division, production of
healthy red blood cells and a healthy nervous system.

It was previously thought that our gut bacteria can synthesise
enough vitamin B12 but this is simply not true. While some vegan
foods have been credited with containing B12 (e.g. fermented
tofu, sea vegetables) these only contain inactive forms that can
actually block the activity of true B12 so should not be used as a
reliable source of B12. Therefore vegans need to consume either
2–3 servings of B12-fortified foods daily or take a daily

supplement. Nutritional yeast flakes are probably the best food source of B12 but check the brand as not all contain sufficient levels. A number of the recipes in this book use nutritional yeast flakes for this reason – they also have a lovely flavour.

Vitamin A

Recent studies suggest that vegans can be deficient in vitamin A. This is because the active form of a vitamin A called retinol is only found in animal products. The body can convert plant-based carotenoids into vitamin A but this can be very inefficient. This means vegans need to ensure they get plenty of these carotenoids daily. Both cooking and adding healthy fats increases the absorption of beta-carotene, so there is some benefit in eating both raw and cooked vegetables. Top vegan foods include carrots, butternut squash, sweet potato, pumpkin, spinach, kale, chicory and other greens.

Iodine

Iodine is an important mineral for metabolism because it helps support optimal thyroid function. In many countries people obtain enough iodine by using iodised salt or by eating fish and dairy products. Iodised salt is not available in the UK so for vegans sea vegetables are one of the best iodine-rich plant foods so try and include these in your diet 1–2 times a week. One of the easiest ways is to soak a handful and add to soups, stews or toss into salads. There is concern that over-consumption of foods like soybeans and raw cruciferous vegetables (e.g. broccoli, cauliflower, cabbage) will interfere with the activity of iodine and adversely affect thyroid function. However as long as your diet is sufficient in iodine there is no reason to avoid soy; cooking cruciferous vegetables also reduces their adverse affects. If you are taking a multivitamin and mineral supplement it may also contain iodine.

Creatine for lean muscle

Creatine is particularly useful to support muscle and fuel recovery after exercise – it's also important for brain function. Creatine is mostly found in skeletal muscle and is made available in a diet of meat and fish. Vegans therefore may benefit from taking a supplement as levels can be low – it's both inexpensive and readily available. Often available as a powder it can be added to smoothies or stirred into water.

Amino acids and protein powders

To support weight loss it is important to ensure a wide spectrum of amino acids and sufficient protein in the diet. For this reason, vegan protein powders are recommended in the *Go Lean Vegan* plan. Some vegans may also benefit from an amino acid formula or a branched chain amino acid formula, especially if they are concerned about digestion and absorption of protein-rich foods, although if you are including protein powders daily, you should be getting sufficient amino acids for your needs.

DO I NEED TO SUPPLEMENT?

Protein, calcium, vitamin B12 and vitamin D often receive particular attention in vegan diets but the truth is that other nutrients could also be less than optimal. As with any diet it's important to include plenty of variety to ensure sufficient nutrients. A combination of factors such as our depleted soils, the storage and transportation of foods as well as the increased stress and nutritional needs of our bodies means it can be useful to take certain nutritional supplements. Consider supplementing with the following:

---> Multi-vitamin and mineral supplement*

---> DHA algae source

---> Vegan protein powders and/or an amino acid formula

---> Additional creatine powder and branched chain amino acids, particularly if exercising frequently

*B12 and iodine should be incorporated in a quality multi-vitamin and mineral formula, but if not take additional supplements

*Calcium and vitamin D supplement – if not included in multi-vitamin formula

The *Go Lean Vegan* Pantry

Before you start the *Go Lean Vegan* programme take time to stock your kitchen with vegan staples and clear out toxic foods that will de-rail your diet. Here are the key staples of a healthy vegan diet:

Beans and Pulses

Beans and pulses are protein-rich and packed with fibre – they also provide key minerals like iron and zinc. While you can buy dried beans and cook them from scratch, this can be time-consuming so to make the plan easier stock up with tins of cooked beans and lentils. Look for those with no salt or sugar added. Dried red split lentils and puy lentils are quick and easy to cook and a very economical source of vegan protein. They don't require soaking and cook in around 20 minutes. Chickpea flour (sometimes referred to as gram flour) is used in a few recipes as it is rich in protein and acts as a great binder to replace eggs.

Sprouted beans are particularly rich in vitamins, minerals and amino acids, and sprouting also helps to improve the digestibility. While you can purchase sprouted beans, grains, nuts and seeds, it's easy to sprout your own at home, especially if you are already in the habit of soaking. You can use a wide-necked glass jar or a sprouter. Soak the beans overnight as above, then rinse and drain. Spread them evenly over the sprouter and rinse 3–4 times a day. Place in a light place but away from direct sunlight. Depending on the type of bean or seed it can take between 1–5 days for the sprouts to be ready. They are ready when the sprouts are the length of the soaked seed. When ready rinse and place in a container in the fridge and use within 2–3 days.

Stock up with:

---> Tins of black beans, butter beans, cannellini beans, kidney beans, mixed soya beans
---> Chickpea (gram) flour
---> Split peas and red lentils
---> Green or puy lentils (tinned or dried)
---> Sprouted beans

Soy Products

There is no doubt that soy is a useful protein source for vegans because it contains all the essential amino acids. Fermented soy products like miso, tamari, natto and tempeh have been staples of Asian cultures for centuries. However, cultivation of the soybean has given rise to many other products, including meat substitutes like textured vegetable protein (TVP), soya cheese, spreads and processed foods like vegan burgers and hotdogs. These processed foods are far removed from traditional soy products and often full of unwanted additives. Keep these foods out of your diet and focus instead on unprocessed options, preferably organic and non-genetically modified.

Soy products can be somewhat controversial as it's a common allergen food and may not be tolerated by everyone. There is also some concern that for people with low thyroid function soy may be problematic. This is because soy and certain other foods contain goitrogens – compounds that have been shown to interfere with thyroid function. However, if your diet is sufficiently rich in iodine, consuming a little soy should not be a problem. Fermenting soy further reduces the activity of goitrogens – another reason for focusing more on fermented soy products. These also contain probiotics and are easier to digest and absorb. You don't have to include soy products in your diet, and although they are included in some of the recipes you can generally replace them with other protein options like beans and pulses.

Tempeh is a fermented soybean product that has a firmer, more meaty texture than tofu – it's also easier to digest and richer in absorbable nutrients. It often comes frozen in blocks (look for it in health food shops or online). In traditional dishes it is often sautéed with vegetables or added to curries. Tofu is readily available and comes in various forms. Silken tofu is available in UHT packets and is soft in texture. It is ideal for blending in smoothies, sauces and desserts, making it an easy way to increase your protein intake. It also has a long shelf life and can be kept in the store cupboard. Firm tofu is usually sold fresh, covered in a little water in packets, so you need to keep it refrigerated. You can also freeze tofu; it gives it a chewy, spongy texture that makes it useful as a meat substitute (freeze in unopened packets then defrost, squeeze out the excess liquid and crumble into dishes). Tofu tastes bland on its own but is delicious marinated in sauces and pan-fried. You can also get smoked tofu, which is equally delicious tossed into cooked dishes and salads. Miso is another fermented product typically added to many Asian dishes. It has a naturally salty flavour and a little goes a long way. Use it in soups and broths to add richness. Tamari soy sauce is a popular fermented soy product and is gluten-free unlike refined processed soy sauce – it also has a richer flavour. Frozen shelled edamame (soybeans) are a great standby; they can be cooked in minutes and make a useful protein boost for salads and stews.

Stock up with:
- Frozen shelled edamame/soya beans
- Firm tofu
- Silken tofu
- Frozen tempeh
- Miso
- Tamari soy sauce

Gluten-free Whole Grains and Starchy Vegetables

These foods are naturally high in fibre and provide protein, iron, zinc and B vitamins. As they are starches, watch your portion sizes (1 serving = 1/3 cup cooked grains or 1/2 cup cooked starchy vegetables) to keep your blood sugar balanced. Potatoes are not included as these are high-glycaemic – a more nutritious option is sweet potato, which you'll find in several of the recipes. Look for bags of fresh or frozen chopped butternut squash, sweet potato and carrot to help save time in the kitchen.

Grains such as quinoa, buckwheat and millet cook very much like rice. Ideally soak these grains in water first and rinse well to improve digestibility. To cook simply place 1 cup of the grain in a pan and cover with 2–3 cups of water. Bring to the boil then reduce the heat and simmer for 15–20 minutes. You can also purchase quinoa, millet and buckwheat flakes, which can be used to replace oats. Rice is another useful grain but choose wholegrain, red rice or black rice, which are slower releasing, high in fibre and a good source of antioxidants and minerals.

Some of the recipes include almond flour and coconut flour – these are readily available in supermarkets, health food shops and online and provide additional protein and fibre in recipes. Teff flour is particularly protein-rich and is delicious made into breads and cookies. It is available in health stores and online.

Stock up with:
- Quinoa, millet and buckwheat (whole grain and flakes)
- Teff flour
- Coconut flour
- Almond flour
- Gluten-free oats
- Sweet potato, carrot, beetroot, pumpkin, parsnip, butternut squash (fresh and frozen)

Nuts and Seeds

Don't be afraid of including nuts and seeds daily. These are rich in healthy fats and protein as well as many valuable minerals like calcium and magnesium. Ideal as a snack they can be added to dishes to further boost the protein content. Choose bags of nuts that are unsalted and that haven't been fried in oils and syrups. Nut butters make an ideal snack spread onto raw crackers, slices of apple or celery sticks but always choose brands without added sugar and salt. Store nut and seed oils in the fridge as they are more vulnerable to heat damage.

Stock up with:
- Almonds and ground almonds
- Cashew nuts
- Brazil nuts
- Pecan nuts
- Hazelnuts
- Macadamia nuts
- Pine nuts
- Coconut products, including desiccated coconut, flakes, yoghurt and milk
- Nut butters (without sugar or sweeteners)
- Tahini paste (sesame seed paste)
- Sesame seeds
- Pumpkin seeds
- Sunflower seeds
- Flaxseed
- Chia seeds

···› Shelled hemp seeds
···› Nut and seed oils (walnut, macadamia, flaxseed)

Vegetables

Vegetables are nutrient-dense and packed with an array of valuable vitamins, minerals and antioxidants, so should form a main part in your meals. Include a wide colourful selection and at least 2–3 cups of leafy green vegetables each day. Make use of bags of frozen vegetables which take little effort to prepare and cook. Stock the pantry with a packet of dried sea vegetables – they have 10–20 times the minerals of those found in land plants. They are an excellent source of minerals such as iodine, calcium, and iron. You can buy bags of mixed sea vegetables, which require minimum soaking before adding to dishes. You can also buy seaweed flakes, which can be sprinkled over dishes. Nori sheets are commonly used in making sushi (see page 179). They can also be eaten directly from the packet by lightly toasting and crumbling onto food. Agar agar flakes are useful as a thickening agent and as an alternative to gelatine. Kelp noodles are also available from health shops and can be used to replace standard noodles in dishes. They are low in carbohydrates and rich in minerals.

Fruits

Include a variety of fresh and frozen fruits, particularly berries, citrus fruits and stone fruits, which tend to be lower-glycemic fruits and packed with protective antioxidants. Don't go over-board with fruit though – limit yourself to two portions a day. Avoid fruit juices, which are too high in sugar and will disrupt blood glucose levels. Lemons and limes are a great addition to dressings and sauces so keep a plentiful supply. For a speedy calcium-rich dressing simply blend a little tahini paste with lemon juice and water and season to taste.

Fermented Foods

If possible try and include fermented foods regularly in your diet. These provide beneficial bacteria to support digestive health and lower inflammation. Most sauerkraut is processed and heat-treated so lacks the beneficial bacteria – if possible choose raw sauerkraut or make your own (see page 239). As well as soy products (see pages 40–42), fermented foods include coconut yoghurt and vegan nut cheese (see recipes on pages 81 and 87).

Non-Dairy Alternatives

Nut and seed milks are ideal alternatives to milk in recipes and can also be added to drinks and smoothies. You can make your own (see page 79) or use shop-bought – choose unsweetened forti-fied brands. While soya milk tends to be higher in protein, it often comes from non-organic, genetically modified soy. If you are consuming soy in the form of tofu and tempeh try and include other milk alternatives such as almond or coconut milk to increase variety in your diet. Tinned coconut milk is ideal added to curries and Asian dishes and makes a useful standby store cupboard ingredient. Nuts and silken tofu can be blended to make creamy sauces and dips to replace creams and cheese in recipes. You can also make your own nut milk and cream and coconut yoghurt (see pages 79–84).

Store Cupboard

Stocking up on pantry essentials before you start the programme will help you stick to the plan and recipes. Many of these ingredients have a long shelf life and will add not only flavour but key nutrients to your dishes too.

Stock up with:
- Tinned tomatoes
- Passata (sieved tomatoes)
- Vegan Worcestershire sauce
- Tomato purée
- Tamari soy sauce
- Harissa paste
- Dijon mustard
- Nutritional yeast flakes – ideally fortified with B12
- Sea salt and black pepper
- Herbs and spices
- Oils (olive, coconut, avocado, nut and seed)
- Balsamic vinegar
- Red wine vinegar
- Rice wine vinegar
- Apple cider vinegar

---⟶ White miso paste
---⟶ Mirin (Japanese rice wine)
---⟶ Pomegranate molasses
---⟶ Bouillon vegan stock powder
---⟶ Sun-dried tomatoes in oil
---⟶ Dried porcini mushrooms

Baking

The plan includes recipes to make your own bars and healthy snacks. Almonds, almond flour and coconut flour are great additions to homemade baked goods, providing more protein and fibre than processed refined flours. Teff flour is equally delicious and particularly rich in protein. Stock up with some vegan protein powders too which are included in some of the recipes – ideally choose one without added sugars. You can also get flavoured powders such as vanilla, chocolate and berry, which are delicious when used in homemade bars, snacks and desserts.

The main sweeteners used in the plan are xylitol and stevia. These are naturally derived rather than artificial sweeteners and do not disrupt blood sugar levels like other sweeteners such as maple syrup. Dark chocolate and cocoa powder is included in some of the recipes. Dark chocolate is a good source of minerals such as magnesium but check the labels as many contain dairy. Choose sugar-free brands to keep the overall sugar content low. Raw cacao is the unprocessed form of cocoa powder and typically richer in antioxidants. It has a milder and slightly sweeter flavour. Vanilla extract is used in some of the recipes – make sure you buy pure vanilla extract without sugars added.

Cooking without eggs

It may feel daunting to bake without eggs but there are many alternatives you can use. Eggs are often used in baking to help with leavening or as a binding agent. They can also be used as a glaze or to thicken sauces. Try some of the following alternatives – each will replace one egg.

→ 1 tbsp agar agar flakes soaked in 2 tbsp hot water to dissolve

→ 1 tbsp soy flour blended with 3 tbsp water

→ 60g silken tofu, blended

→ ½ banana, mashed

→ ¼ cup apple purée

→ ¼ cup pumpkin purée

→ ¼ cup coconut or soya yoghurt

→ ¼ cup cooked sweet potato or butternut squash purée

→ 2 tbsp potato flour, arrowroot or cornflour

→ 2 tbsp chickpea flour blended with 3 tbsp water

→ 1 tbsp ground flaxseed soaked in 3 tbsp water for 10 minutes

→ 1 tbsp chia seeds soaked in 3 tbsp water for 10 minutes

→ 1 tbsp pysllium husks soaked in 3 tbsp water for 10 minutes

→ 3 tbsp chickpea juice (the soaking liquid from a can of cooked chickpeas) known as aquafaba

Drinks

Your body is made mostly of water and it is crucial to stay hydrated throughout the day. Water is best so aim to drink pure fresh water – 6–8 glasses a day is a useful guide. Remember too that often people mistake hunger for thirst. So before you reach for a snack have a glass of water instead. If you feel sluggish in the morning squeeze a little fresh lemon juice in warm water and drink before breakfast.

If your urine is dark coloured you aren't drinking enough water. It should be the colour of pale straw. Equally if you are prone to constipation make sure you drink enough. If you can filter your own water and take it with you when you go out then this is a good option. If you prefer warm drinks then herbal teas, green tea or dandelion coffee (a natural alternative to coffee) are all great options. Green tea is rich in antioxidants, boosts concentration and has been shown to support metabolism and fat burning. If you are exercising regularly include a glass of coconut water pre- or post-workout – it is rich in electrolytes (sodium, potassium and magnesium) to help hydrate the body quickly. But stick to just one glass a day as it is still quite high in carbohydrates.

Useful Equipment

Before you embark on the *Go Lean Vegan* programme it's important to get your kitchen ready, and that means making sure you have the right equipment as well as a supply of healthy foods. You should already have most of the basic equipment you need, but here are some additional pieces of kit that you may find useful.

Food processor – a great way to speed up preparation. Can be used to grate and finely chop ingredients.

Blender – a high-speed blender is particularly useful for making your own soups, smoothies, nut drinks and even instant ice creams. For smaller quantities such as salad dressings and sauces a Nutribullet or mini chopper is a good option.

Spiraliser – a popular and inexpensive kitchen gadget that is fabulous for making vegetable noodles and finely shredded vegetables to add to salads and other dishes.

Mandoline – useful for very thin slicing of vegetables and fruits, particularly good homemade crisps.

Dehydrator – this is not at all essential but if you love making your own seed crackers, vegetable and kale crisps then you may consider investing in one. A dehydrator slowly removes the moisture from food making it crisp and chewy. If you don't have a dehydrator you can still make kale crisps and crackers in an oven at its lowest setting.

Nut bag – this is a straining bag that can be used for making your own nut and seed milks, although you can strain your milk using a fine sieve, cheesecloth or even a pair of clean stockings.

Sprouter – if you find beans and grains easier to digest sprouted then you may wish to invest in a sprouter. These vary in size but can be very inexpensive.

Go Lean Vegan
Tips for Success

The key to success on any diet plan is to be prepared – this will help you stick to your goals and make you less likely to give in to cravings. Clever shopping and smart cooking can make all the difference.

Shopping Tips: Going Organic

The *Go Lean Vegan* diet is focused around a diet rich in fruits and vegetables. Unfortunately, we also know that many fruits and vegetables can be contaminated with pesticides. For this reason, it is recommended to switch to as much organic produce as possible.

Every year the Environmental Working Group's (EWG) annual Shopper's Guide highlights the fruits and vegetables most likely to be contaminated (the 'Dirty List') and those that are considered the least likely to be contaminated by pesticides (the 'Clean 15'). If it works within your budget, the EWG recommends buying organic whenever possible – the more organic produce you include in your diet the better. However not only can organic produce be more expensive, it may not always be available so if you can only afford a little organic produce then focus on buying those from the Dirty List, as these are most heavily contaminated.

The Dirty List

Apples	Sweet peppers
Peaches	Cucumbers
Nectarines	Cherry tomatoes
Strawberries	Sugar snap peas
Grapes	Potatoes
Celery	Hot peppers
Spinach	Kale/collard greens

The Clean Fifteen

Avocados	Papayas
Sweetcorn	Kiwi fruits
Pineapples	Aubergines
Cabbage	Grapefruit
Sweet peas (frozen)	Cantaloupe
Onions	Cauliflower
Asparagus	Sweet potatoes
Mangoes	

Cooking Smart

Not everyone loves cooking or feels they have the time to spend hours in the kitchen. The recipes included in this plan are quick and easy to prepare, but if you find time is short then take time at the weekend to prepare some of the dishes for the week ahead. You can also double up the recipes and store in the fridge or freezer. Many will keep for several days in the fridge and you can also use leftovers from the evening meal for lunch the next day saving time and money. Most of the recipes can also be frozen in batches.

Other time saving tips:

---> Keep tins of cooked beans and lentils in the store cupboard – they make a fantastic simple protein snack or addition to a salad

---> Batch cook – when cooking lentils double the batch. Once cooked you can store them in containers in the fridge for 3–4 days or freeze in bags for up to 3 months

---> Get soaking – if you want to make your own nut milks or yoghurts get into the habit of soaking nuts overnight. Remember you can rinse them and store them in the fridge safely for 2–3 days before using – they can also be frozen

---> When you have over-ripe fruit simply cut up and freeze for using in ice creams or smoothies

---> If you don't have time to cook your own quinoa you can buy pre-cooked pouches which can be added to dishes instantly – to work out how much to use, as a general rule of thumb, just double the dry raw weight in a recipe

---> Cut up raw vegetables such as cucumber, carrot, red pepper and celery and keep in sealed containers in the fridge for an instant snack

⋯⋗ When using your spiraliser make up double and store the additional vegetable noodles in a container in the fridge for use the next day

⋯⋗ Make up simple mixed salads and store in the fridge to form the basis of a meal when time is short

⋯⋗ Keep a couple of salad dressings in the fridge or simply drizzle a little lemon juice, tamari or apple cider vinegar over meals to liven up flavours

⋯⋗ Make up a couple of the dips in this book and store in the fridge for an easy addition to a meal or snack – they also freeze well

⋯⋗ Keep a jar of nut butter in the fridge for spreading on vegetable sticks if you get hungry

⋯⋗ Make use of frozen bags of vegetables – simply steam and add to your meal

⋯⋗ Keep bags of frozen fruits for desserts, for making your own instant ice cream or for using in smoothies. Peel and cut up ripe bananas and freeze in containers

⋯⋗ Tins of chopped tomatoes and passata can quickly be cooked up into a tangy tomato sauce with the addition of chopped onion, garlic and a dash of apple cider vinegar

⋯⋗ If time is short in the morning use one of the smoothie recipes and assemble the ingredients in a blender the night before and store in the fridge overnight

⋯⋗ Get roasting – if you are roasting vegetables for one of the recipes add some more to use in the Roasted Root Hummus (see page 244) or for adding to soups and stews

Soaking Nuts, Seeds and Pseudo Grains

Soaking nuts and seeds and pseudo grains like quinoa and buckwheat can be useful to improve their digestion. Nuts and seeds naturally contain enzyme inhibitors, which can make them more difficult to digest. By soaking them before using you can help break down these inhibitors as well as reducing any bitterness. The easiest way to do this is simply to place the nuts and seeds in a bowl, cover with cold water and leave to soak for at least 2–3 hours, ideally overnight. Rinse and drain thoroughly before using. Quinoa and other pseudo grains should be soaked in cold water for at least 30 minutes before using. Rinse and drain thoroughly and then cook as directed in the recipe.

Snacks on the Go

During the programme you're going to be getting used to thinking more mindfully about the food you are eating and that includes snacking. Many people fail to lose weight because they end up giving in to snacks even if they are not really hungry. Snacks are included on the plan but remember that these are optional. Do not snack if you are really not hungry.

However, there may be times when snacks can be helpful especially if you are constantly on the go or work away from home a lot. If that is the case you may need to think ahead and pack some healthy options with you – many of the recipes are designed to be portable. Always remember to carry a bottle of water too as thirst can often be mistaken for hunger.

There are plenty of healthy snack options in the pages that follow and you will find your own favourites but here's an example of some simple portable ideas.

Savoury options

⟶ Bags of mixed nuts and seeds

⟶ Tins of cooked beans

⟶ Prepared salad pots

⟶ Bags of prepared carrots, celery sticks, cucumber slices

⟶ Containers of hummus or other dips (see pages 242–245)

⟶ Spicy Crunchy Chickpeas (see page 245)

⟶ Buffalo Cauliflower and Broccoli Bites (see page 248)

⟶ Pots of raw sauerkraut (see page 239)

⟶ Sweet Potato Crisps (see page 250)

⟶ Pizza Kale Crisps (see page 256)

⟶ Flaxseed and Chia Seed Crackers (see page 258)

⟶ Slices of Vegan Seeded Bread (see page 124)

⟶ Pot of nut butter to spread on crackers

Sweet options

⟶ Bags of sliced apple or satsumas

⟶ Cinnamon Trail Mix (see page 254)

⟶ Chocolate Buckwheat Nibbles (see page 260)

⟶ Pot of Pecan Nut and Pumpkin Butter to spread on apple slices (see page 252)

⟶ Coconut Yoghurt (see page 81)

⟶ Chocolate Orange Pot (see page 265)

⟶ Superberry Protein Balls (see page 274)

⟶ Grab-and-Go Vanilla and Chocolate Chip Protein Bars (see page 105)

···❯ Vegan Protein Chocolate Brownies (see page 276)

···❯ Apricot Chia Energy Balls (see page 278)

···❯ Slices of Teff Chocolate Bread (see page 284)

···❯ Raspberry Almond Muffins (see page 280)

···❯ Protein Smoothies (see pages 91–93)

···❯ Protein Berry Mug Cake (see page 286)

The 30-Day Programme

Over the pages that follow you will find detailed week-by-week meal plans that have been specifically devised to make the programme as easy as possible to follow. Being prepared is important to getting the most out of the 30-Day Programme. Before you launch in to it take time to identify your health and weight loss goals and set an official date to start the programme. Follow this checklist to help you prepare:

···⟶ Weigh yourself and measure your waist and hip size so you can monitor your progress

···⟶ Identify your health and weight loss goals and write them down. Keeping a journal as you diet can help you stick to the plan and make you notice real results

···⟶ Clear your kitchen of processed foods, sugary foods and sweeteners

···⟶ Stock your kitchen, fridge and freezer with real, unprocessed vegan foods and make sure you have the ingredients you need for the first few days of the plan to give you time to prepare (see the shopping lists on pages 291–300)

···⟩ If needed, start soaking nuts and seeds or grains for using in recipes

···⟩ Read through the recipes and plan so you are familiar with what you will be eating each day. Purchase the supplements, including protein powders, to support healthy weight loss. Spend the weekend before you start cooking a few dishes to store in the fridge or freezer

The Basics

A nutrient-dense diet is the foundation of the 30-day programme. Over the next 30 days you will be avoiding the following foods. Keeping off these foods will not only help you get thinner but you will feel healthier and more energised. And just as importantly, you will be including a wide variety of wonderful plant-based foods.

What to avoid

Sugars – in all forms (with the exception of xylitol and stevia)

Alcohol – this disrupts blood sugar, adds excess calories and often reduces any resolve to stick to the plan

Caffeine – regular tea and coffee can disrupt blood sugar levels so switch to herbal teas, dandelion coffee, green tea

Processed and refined foods – this includes breads, pasta, wraps, biscuits and cakes (even gluten-free products). Avoid processed soy products too

Gluten – wheat, barley, rye, spelt are inflammatory in our diet and eliminating them will help improve digestion, blood sugar balance and weight loss

What to include

Slow-releasing low-glycaemic vegetables – fill your plate with these at each meal and choose organic where possible

Sea vegetables – includes nori, wakame, dulse and sea vegetable mixes

Starchy vegetables and gluten-free grains – including brown and red rice, quinoa, millet, buckwheat, teff, sweet potato, sweet-corn, butternut squash, pumpkin, parsnips, carrots and beetroot

Beans and pulses – include 3–4 servings a day of lentils, tinned beans, chickpeas, edamame, tofu, split peas

Nuts and seeds – useful for weight loss, they make a great snack and provide protein as well as fibre and healthy fats

Healthy fats – these include the nuts and seeds above but also olives, avocados and healthy oils (olive, coconut, walnut, hemp seed etc.)

Fermented foods – aim to include these regularly. Before you start the plan I would really recommend either purchasing some raw sauerkraut or making your own

Fruit – your total fruit intake should be up to 2 portions a day. Focus on slower-releasing fruits like berries, citrus fruits, stone fruit (plums, peaches, nectarines), apples and pears

Occasional treats – this could include 1–2 squares of dark choco-late or a recipe like the Chocolate Buckwheat Nibbles (see page 260). Dried fruit is only included in protein snacks and should not be eaten as a snack on its own

Herbs and spices – use liberally in dishes. They are powerful anti-oxidants and natural anti-inflammatories. They are also a fabu-lous way to add flavour to dishes

Water – keep the body hydrated with 6–8 glasses of water a day, plus herbal teas and green tea

Get your portions right

People often put on weight because their portions are far too big – use these guidelines to help plan your own meals. The following are all equivalent to 1 serving:

- → Grains: 60g (1/3 cup) cooked weight
- → Beans and pulses: 80–130g (½–3/4 cup) cooked weight (about half a tin)
- → Nuts and seeds/nut butter: 2 tbsp
- → Fruit: 1 apple or pear, ½ grapefruit, around ½ cup berries
- → Starchy vegetables: ½ cup cooked weight
- → Other vegetables: unlimited – try to include 1–2 cups of leafy greens daily
- → Fats and oils: 1 tbsp oil, ¼ avocado, 30g olives

Building the perfect plate

Forget counting calories – it's the quality of your calories that's important. Focusing on the balance of your plate can help you lose weight and boost metabolism. The *Go Lean Vegan* plate looks like this:

- → 50% of the plate should be colourful slow-releasing vegetables. Try to include at least two or three different types and at least one should be leafy greens like kale, broccoli, spinach – this can include raw salads and steamed or roasted vegetables
- → 30–40% should be protein-rich vegan foods like beans and pulses or a combination of some beans and nuts or seeds – this will ensure sufficient protein and healthy fats

⇢ 10–20% should be a little cooked gluten-free whole grain (like quinoa or buckwheat) or half a cup of starchy vegetables such as sweet potato or beetroot. This is optional as beans and legumes also contain carbohydrate. For a faster weight loss result leave these off the plate.

Eat at regular times through the day and avoid eating 2–3 hours before bedtime to support digestive health and balance blood sugar. New research suggests that it's not just what we eat that is important for weight loss but when we eat. Leave at least 12–14 hours overnight of not eating to allow the body to digest food and support healthy blood sugar – so eat your evening meal at 7 p.m and nothing further until 7 a.m.

The Importance of Exercise and Lifestyle

Exercise

There's no doubt that if you want to achieve a lean, healthy body, you need to engage in regular exercise – it will help to boost weight loss, ditch belly fat and improve blood sugar balance. Exercise also plays an important role in improving long-term health, cardiovascular health, bone health, muscle mass and mood – to name a few. But the activity must be regular and frequent, and a combination of both aerobic exercise and resistance (weight) training is likely to be the most beneficial. If you're looking to incorporate health changes long-term, then make exercise fun and include it as a key part of your daily routine. Choose a form of exercise you enjoy. You should be looking to include a minimum of 30 minutes of vigorous exercise every day (walking, running, cycling, dance, swimming etc.). Ideally increase this to 60 minutes as your fitness allows. If time is short, wake up an hour earlier to fit it in. This has the added benefit of kick-starting the day. Some studies also suggest that exercise before breakfast may increase fat burning.

The type of exercise you do is also important. Studies have consistently shown that to boost metabolism and encourage fat burning interval training – short bursts of high intensity exercise – is particularly effective. Compared to resistance training (weights) and traditional cardio, sprint intervals increase resting energy expenditure the most. Most of the increased expenditure appears to come from fat oxidation – this means improved fat burning. Best of all, the increased expenditure following sprinting does not lead to increased food intake – so it should not make you hungrier either. Aim to incorporate high-intensity interval-work two to three times a week. This could include running fast on a treadmill or outdoors (5–6 times) for short bursts (e.g. 30 seconds) in between gentle jogging or walking or similar sprints on a stationary bicycle for example.

Strength training is equally important as it helps maintain and build muscle. Whether you use a gym, exercise machines, home weights or participate in certain sports like yoga, Pilates or martial arts, aim to include strength work at least three times a week. Strength training increases resting metabolic rate over the short and long term.

Lifestyle

There are other many lifestyle factors that can affect your weight. When we are facing ongoing stress our levels of the stress hormone cortisol can become elevated. This appears to lead to a drop in metabolic rate as well as disrupting blood sugar levels. Another factor is that often when we feel stressed we find ourselves reaching for the biscuit tin for a quick pick-me-up and following a healthy eating programme can be difficult. Address any ongoing stress and take time each day to unwind and relax.

Poor sleep can also have profound effects on our hormones, mood and blood sugar balance. Appetite can also be increased due to sleep deprivation, meaning it can be harder to stick to a diet. Don't underestimate the importance of sleep. It's SO important to get your 7–8 hours per night.

Keeping Healthy for Life

When the programme is over and you have achieved your health and weight loss goals, it may be tempting to switch back to your old eating patterns. Resist the urge, however, as the nutrition principles outlined here are for life. This means keeping sugar, refined carbohydrates, processed foods and ready meals to a minimum. Keep to the perfect plate balance, focusing on protein, slow-releasing carbohydrates from vegetables and healthy fats at each meal. You may find you can increase the amount of starchy carbohydrates from grains like quinoa, buckwheat, millet or vegetables like carrot, sweet potato and beetroot. If you exercise regularly you may wish to include an additional snack post workout to support your fitness programme.

If you are sticking to a vegan style of eating, then you will also need to continue with the supplements. This will ensure all your nutritional needs are being met for your long-term health.

Meal Plans

WEEK ONE: Fast Track

During the first week I have kept the recipes simple to allow you to transition easily into the plan and get results. For example, you will be making smoothies for breakfast as well as dishes that can be eaten over a couple of days (see the action points over and aim to get organised the weekend before you start the plan). This reduces time spent in the kitchen, as well as making it easy for you to consume sufficient protein over the week, which will boost results. The only fruits you will be consuming this week are in the protein shakes – keeping the carbohydrate intake lower will give you speedier results.

Week 1 Meal Planner

	Day 1	Day 2	Day 3
Breakfast	Protein Greens Smoothie	Berry Beauty Cream Shake	Fat Burner Smoothie
Lunch	Broccoli Coconut Cream Soup; mixed salad	Creamy Caesar-style Kale Salad (make enough for tomorrow); 130g cooked tofu or beans	Creamy Caesar-style Kale Salad; 130g Spiced Crunchy Chickpeas
Snack	Chocolate Orange Pot	30g Chocolate Buckwheat Nibbles	2 tbsp Roasted Root Hummus; celery or cucumber sticks
Dinner	Sweet Potato and Lentil Moussaka (make enough for tomorrow); steamed greens (fill half the plate)	Sweet Potato and Lentil Moussaka; mixed salad	Almond Pad Thai (make enough for tomorrow)

Action points

--→ Make up the Broccoli Coconut Soup – you will need 3 portions (keep in the fridge or freeze portions)

--→ Roast 150g carrots to make the hummus

--→ Roast chickpeas and store in an airtight container

--→ Make up the Chocolate Buckwheat Nibbles and store in an airtight container

--→ Make up the Chocolate Orange Pots and store in the fridge or freezer

--→ Make the Moussaka for Days 1 and 2 (any extra can be frozen in containers)

--→ Remember the snacks are optional – if you are not hungry then skip them but if you are exercising regularly save them for a post-exercise refuel.

Day 4	Day 5	Day 6	Day 7
Breakfast Morning Pick-Me-Up	Cinnamon Peanut Butter Shake	Protein Chocolate Latte	Breakfast Morning Pick-Me-Up (or other smoothie)
Almond Pad Thai	4 Pea Falafels with Tzatziki; mixed salad	Broccoli Coconut Cream Soup; mixed salad	Broccoli Coconut Cream Soup; mixed salad
Chocolate Orange Pot	30g Chocolate Buckwheat Nibbles	Chocolate Orange Pot	100g coconut yoghurt
4 Pea Falafels with Tzatziki (save the rest for tomorrow); 2 tbsp Roasted Root Hummus, steamed vegetables	Roasted Cauliflower and Pistachio Tabbouleh (make enough for tomorrow); 150g cooked butterbeans; green salad	Roasted Cauliflower and Pistachio Tabbouleh; green salad; 150g cooked beans or tofu	Pesto and Caramelised Red Onion Pizza; steamed vegetables and/or mixed salad

WEEK TWO

Hopefully you will have noticed a weight loss of around 1–1½kg during the first week. This week you will introduce a few additional breakfast options to give you more variety. If time is short in the morning prepare the evening before or simply switch back to the smoothies. Over the weekend take time to make up some of the dishes that can be frozen or stored in the fridge for 3–4 days.

Week 2 Meal Planner

	Day 1	Day 2	Day 3
Breakfast	Tofu Vegetable Scramble	50g Nutty Pear Granola Clusters with almond milk	Protein Chocolate Latte
Lunch	Pesto and Caramelised Red Onion Pizza; mixed salad; Red Cabbage and Apple Sauerkraut	One Pot Spiced Vegetable Tagine; green salad	Spiced Lentil Soup (make 2 servings); mixed salad
Snack	Celery sticks with 2 tbsp Creamy Nacho Dip	70g blueberries and a handful of nuts	Cucumber slices with 2 tbsp Creamy Nacho Dip
Dinner	One Pot Spiced Vegetable Tagine (make enough for tomorrow); 30g quinoa, dry weight (cook enough for the Miso Quinoa Bowl tomorrow)	Miso Quinoa Bowl; mixed salad	Cauliflower and Tofu Fried Rice (make enough for tomorrow); green salad

Action points

···→ Make up the Nutty Pear Granola and store in an airtight container

···→ Make up the Creamy Nacho Dip and store in the fridge

···→ Make up the Spiced Lentil Soup – you will need 2 servings

···→ Make Grab-and-Go Vanilla and Chocolate Chip Protein Bars and keep in the fridge or freezer

···→ Cut up celery sticks and cucumbers and store in a plastic box in the fridge

Day 4	Day 5	Day 6	Day 7
Chia Layered Pudding (keep one for tomorrow)	Chia Layered Pudding	Grab-and-Go Vanilla and Chocolate Chip Protein Bar	50g Nutty Pear Granola Clusters with almond milk
Cauliflower and Tofu Fried Rice; green salad	Spiced Lentil Soup; mixed salad	Waldorf Salad with Smoked Tofu	Stuffed Peppers
Small bowl of Red Cabbage and Apple Sauerkraut	Grab-and-Go Vanilla and Chocolate Chip Protein Bar	Berry Beauty Cream Shake	Grab-and-Go Vanilla and Chocolate Chip Protein Bar
Vegan Bolognese with Vegetable Noodles (make enough for tomorrow)	Vegan Bolognese with Vegetable Noodles	Stuffed Peppers (make enough for tomorrow); mixed salad	Vegan Meatballs with Barbecue Tomato Sauce; steamed broccoli

WEEK THREE

By now you should be feeling more confident about eating and planning vegan meals. This week we include a few more baked goods that can be stored in the fridge or freezer for easy options when time is short. Many of the staples you will still have in your cupboards.

Week 3 Meal Planner

	Day 1	Day 2	Day 3
Breakfast	Grab-and-Go Vanilla and Chocolate Chip Protein Bar	Coconut Yoghurt with Berry Jam	Protein Greens Smoothie
Lunch	Noodle Pot Salad	Fennel, Tomato and Bean Crumble Bake	Tex Mex Burger with Spicy Chilli Dressing; Creamy Celeriac Slaw; mixed salad
Snack	1 slice of Teff Chocolate bread	Pizza Kale Crisps	Grab-and-Go Vanilla and Chocolate Chip Protein Bar
Dinner	Fennel, Tomato and Bean Crumble Bake; mixed salad	Tex Mex Burger with Spicy Chilli Dressing (make enough for tomorrow); Creamy Celeriac Slaw; mixed salad	Thai Vegetable Curry with Cauliflower Rice

Action points

⇢ Make up the Fennel, Tomato and Bean Crumble Bake
  – keep in the fridge for 3–4 days or freeze

⇢ Make up some coconut yoghurt (or use shop-bought)

⇢ Prepare the Creamy Celeriac Slaw

⇢ Make up the Pizza Kale Crisps and store in an airtight container

⇢ Make the Tex Mex Burgers with Spicy Chilli dressing
  – these can be stored in the fridge for 3-4 days or the
  burgers can be frozen

⇢ Make a batch of Flaxseed and Chia Seed Crackers –
  these will store in an airtight container

⇢ Make the Chocolate Teff Bread. You can also slice this
  and freeze portions

Day 4	Day 5	Day 6	Day 7
Protein Berry Mug Cake	Overnight Bircher Protein Bowl	Protein Banana Pancakes with 2 tbsp coconut yoghurt	2 Veggie Fritters; handful of cherry tomatoes, wilted spinach
Ramen Tofu Noodle Bowl (make enough for tomorrow); mixed salad	Ramen Tofu Noodle Bowl; mixed salad	Warm Lentil, Tomato and Olive Salad with Tahini Dressing (make enough for tomorrow); green salad	Warm Lentil, Tomato and Olive Salad with Tahini Dressing; green salad
1 Flaxseed and Chia Seed Cracker with 1 tsp tahini	1 Flaxseed and Chia Seed Cracker with 1 tsp tahini	50g Spiced Crunchy Chickpeas	Vegan Protein Chocolate Brownie
Coconut Dahl with Wilted Greens; 30g quinoa, dry weight (cook extra for the tacos tomorrow)	Quinoa Black Bean Tacos; mixed salad	Asian-marinated Tofu Skewers with Cucumber Salad; steam green vegetables	Courgette Carbonara; mixed salad

WEEK FOUR

This week you should be feeling more confident in your body and the results you are achieving. To help shift additional pounds this week make sure you include plenty of protein to stabilise blood sugar and keep you energised throughout the day – protein smoothies and snacks are ideal post workout snacks if you are increasing your exercise levels.

Week 4 Meal Planner

	Day 1	Day 2	Day 3
Breakfast	2 slices of Vegan Seeded Bread with 1 tbsp Pecan Nut and Pumpkin Butter	Layered Berry, Yoghurt and Granola Pot	Protein Greens Smoothie
Lunch	Middle Eastern Chickpea Salad; salad greens	Tamari Marinated Mushrooms and Mixed Bean Salad	Easy Chilli Pot; cauliflower rice and green salad
Snack	Cinnamon Peanut Butter Shake	Superberry Protein Ball	Apple slices with 1 tbsp Pecan Nut and Pumpkin Butter
Dinner	Black Bean, Shiitake and Red Pepper Stir-Fry; green salad	Easy Chilli Pot (make enough for tomorrow); cauliflower rice	Pomegranate-glazed Aubergine Lentil Salad (make enough for tomorrow)

Action points

...⇒ Make up some Pecan Nut and Pumpkin Butter to store in the fridge

...⇒ Make up the Superberry Protein Balls and keep in the fridge or freezer

...⇒ Make the Vegan Seeded Bread – you can slice and freeze if you wish

...⇒ Make up the Roasted Red Pepper and Bean Dip

...⇒ Make up the Green Energy Soup and freeze if wished

> Shopping lists: I have created shopping lists for all the meal plans and recipes on pages 291–300

Day 4	Day 5	Day 6	Day 7
2 Veggie Fritters with Yoghurt Herb Sauce (save the rest for tomorrow)	Coconut Quinoa Bowl with Blueberries	Tofu Vegetable Scramble	2 slices of Vegan Seeded Bread with 1 tbsp Pecan Nut and Pumpkin Butter
Pomegranate-glazed Aubergine Lentil Salad; salad leaves	Veggie Fritters with Yoghurt Herb Sauce; mixed salad	Vegan Bolognese with Vegetable Noodles	Vietnamese Tofu Salad
Superberry Protein Ball	Vegan Protein Chocolate Brownie	Protein Banana Ice Cream	Protein Banana Ice Cream
Pesto-stuffed Portobello Mushrooms; steamed vegetables and mixed salad	Vegan Bolognese with Vegetable Noodles (make enough for tomorrow)	Buckwheat, Mushroom and Spinach Risotto (make enough for tomorrow); mixed salad	Buckwheat, Mushroom and Spinach Risotto; mixed salad

RECIPES
Vegan Pantry

Nut or Seed Milk

It's incredibly simple to make your own nut or seed milk and the beauty is that you can vary the flavours according to your personal preference. You can use any nut or seed but cashews, almonds and macadamia nuts are the most popular as they create a wonderful creamy texture. The best seeds to use are hemp and sunflower. Always use raw unsalted nuts and seeds.

PREPARATION TIME: 5 minutes, plus soaking
MAKES 750–950ml

125g raw unsalted nuts or seeds
500–750ml water
Stevia, xylitol or vanilla extract, to taste (optional)

First soak the nuts in a bowl of cold water for at least 6 hours, preferably overnight.

Rinse and drain the nuts and add to a high-speed blender. Add the measured water – as a rough guide you will need 2–3 cups of water for every 1 cup of nuts, depending how thick and creamy you want your milk. Blend on high speed for about 1 minute. Add a little stevia or vanilla extract to sweeten if desired.

Strain the mixture into a jug or bowl through a fine sieve or use a nut bag or cheesecloth placed in a sieve. Transfer to a bottle or jar and keep in the fridge for 2–3 days. You can also freeze nut milk for up to 1 month.

Per 250ml (almond milk): 219 kcal; 7.5g protein; 19.9g fat; 1.6g saturated fat; 2.3g carbohydrates; 1.4g sugars

Coconut Yoghurt

Making your own coconut yoghurt is surprisingly simple and is so much cheaper than shop-bought versions. For ease get yourself an inexpensive electric yoghurt-maker which will keep your yoghurt at a constant temperature as it ferments. Alternatively you can use a Thermos flask. You will need to introduce beneficial bacteria into the coconut milk, which you can do by either using shop-bought coconut yoghurt or by using probiotic capsules.

PREPARATION TIME: 10 minutes
FERMENTING TIME: 8–24 hours
SERVES 8

2 x 400ml tins full-fat coconut milk
1 tbsp agar agar flakes
Contents of 2 probiotic capsules or 2 tbsp natural coconut
yoghurt

Place the coconut milk and agar agar flakes in a pan. Bring to the boil then reduce the heat and simmer for about 2–3 minutes, stirring until the flakes have dissolved in the milk.

Take off the heat and allow the milk to cool to room temperature. Stir in your starter – either the coconut yoghurt or the contents of the probiotic capsules. Place the yoghurt in a yoghurt-maker or

Thermos flask and allow it to ferment for at least 8 hours or over-night – ideally for 24 hours. Stir it occasionally.

Once the yoghurt is ready place it in the fridge to allow the mixture to firm up. This will keep in the fridge for 5–7 days

Per 100g serving: 173 kcal; 1.3g protein; 16.9g fat; 14.6g saturated fat; 3.1g carbohydrates; 1.9g sugars

Nut Cream

This is delicious served with a little fresh fruit as a snack or breakfast option. You can also flavour this with a little vanilla, fresh juice or cocoa powder and use it to top cakes and brownies. Any nuts can be used but almonds, macadamia nuts and cashew nuts are particularly good. I like to flavour the cream with orange juice but for a plain option simply use water. For a sweeter option use a pinch of stevia.

PREPARATION TIME: 10 minutes, plus soaking
SERVES 6

125g raw unsalted cashew nuts
Juice of 1 orange or 3–4 tbsp water
1 tsp vanilla extract (optional)
Pinch of granulated stevia (optional)

Soak the cashew nuts in cold water for at least 2 hours, preferably overnight.

Rinse and drain the nuts and place in a food processor or high-speed blender with half the orange juice or water and vanilla extract, if using. Process until creamy, adding the remaining liquid as needed to create a thick, creamy consistency. Taste and add a pinch of stevia, if liked.

Store in the fridge in an airtight container for up to 4–5 days.

Per 2 tbsp: 124 kcal; 3.8g protein; 10g fat; 2g saturated fat; 4.4g carbohydrates; 19.9g sugars

Tangy Garlic Mayo

This is such an easy recipe and makes delicious alternative to mayonnaise. Use a spoonful over salads, beans or as a dip with vegetable sticks. I've made it tangy with the addition of apple cider vinegar and tamari but you can play around with the flavours – try adding a little lime juice with the garlic and water for a slightly sour flavour. You can also blend in some sun-dried tomatoes or roasted red pepper.

PREPARATION TIME: 10 minutes, plus soaking
SERVES 8

125g raw unsalted cashew nuts
2 tbsp apple cider vinegar
1 tbsp lemon juice
1 tbsp tamari soy sauce
1 garlic clove, chopped
1 tsp xylitol (optional)
Sea salt and black pepper

Soak the cashew nuts in cold water for at least 2 hours, preferably overnight.

Rinse and drain the nuts and place with all the ingredients in a blender or Nutribullet. Add 3–4 tablespoons of water – just enough to blend – and process until thick and creamy. Season to taste with salt and pepper.

Keep in an airtight container in the fridge for up to 1 week.

Red Pepper Ranch Dressing

Add 1 roasted red pepper from a jar and ¼ red onion, plus a handful of fresh parsley and dill.

Lime Sour Cream

Replace the vinegar and lemon juice with the juice of 2 limes, omit the tamari and increase the garlic to 2 cloves – delicious served with beans and tacos.

Per 2 tbsp (30g): 93 kcal; 2.9g protein; 7.5g fat; 1.5g saturated fat; 3.4g carbohydrates; 0.9g sugars

Vegan Nut Cheese

This is another great fermented food that is very simple to make. I like to use a combination of cashew and macadamia nuts but you could use all cashew if preferred. Experiment with different flavours – try stirring in fresh herbs or garlic and spices, depending on what you like.

PREPARATION TIME: 10 minutes, plus soaking
FERMENTING TIME: 24 hours
MAKES about 260g

80g cashew nuts
80g macadamia nuts
Juice of ½ lemon
1 tbsp tamari soy sauce
3 tbsp nutritional yeast flakes
½ tsp sea salt
Pinch of black pepper
Contents of 2 probiotic capsules (optional)

Additional flavours
2 tbsp chopped fresh herbs
1 tsp garlic or onion powder
1–2 tsp ground cumin powder, smoked paprika or cayenne
    pepper

Soak the cashew and macadamia nuts in cold water for at least 2 hours, preferably overnight.

Rinse and drain the nuts and place in a high-speed blender with all the other ingredients and process until smooth, adding 3–4 tablespoons water to blend. Add any additional flavours, if using, and blend briefly again.

Line a sieve or colander with a piece of muslin or cheesecloth and set over a bowl to catch the liquid. Spoon in the mixture then fold the cloth over the mixture or twist the ends of the cloth to seal it. Place a small plate over the top in the sieve and place a tin or weight on the top. Leave it for at least 24 hours at room temperature to allow it to ferment.

Store in the fridge for up to 2 weeks. If you want you can shape the cheese into logs and roll it in a mixture of chopped fresh herbs or spices to coat.

Per serving: 279 kcal; 7.1g protein; 25.3g fat; 4.1g saturated fat; 5.8g carbohydrates; 1.8g sugars

Smoothies and Pick-Me-Up Drinks

These power-packed smoothies are designed to energise the body and keep you feeling full. Use them as a quick breakfast option on the go, to fast track your weight loss and as a post-workout snack.

Protein Greens Smoothie

Perfect as a breakfast option on the go or as a post-workout refuel. Blending the greens with vitamin C-rich kiwi fruit also helps the body absorb iron more effectively. The spirulina is optional but is an excellent source of additional vegan protein, as well as energising magnesium. The seeds provide additional fibre to keep you feeling fuller for longer.

PREPARATION TIME: 5 minutes
SERVES 1

1 kiwi fruit, peeled
½ pear, chopped
Large handful of spinach leaves
1 tsp chia seeds
1 scoop (30g) vanilla protein powder
½ tsp spirulina powder (optional)
250ml water

Simply place all the ingredients in a high-speed blender and process until smooth.

Per serving: 196 kcal; 25.5g protein; 3.9g fat; 0.1g saturated fat; 19.4g carbohydrates; 16.4g sugars

Berry Beauty Cream Shake

Berries are a fabulous skin booster, being rich in protective anti-oxidants and vitamin C to promote the production of collagen. They are also rich in fibre and are low glycemic, helping to keep your blood sugar balanced throughout the day. The tahini gives this smoothie a lovely creamy texture as well as providing calcium, protein and healthy fats.

PREPARATION TIME: 5 minutes
SERVES 1

Large handful (100g) of mixed berries, fresh or frozen
1 tbsp (10g) tahini paste
1 scoop (30g) vanilla protein powder
1 tsp flaxseed oil or Omega blend oil
250–300ml water

Simply blend all the ingredients in a high-speeder blender until smooth.

Per serving: 236 kcal; 26.1g protein; 12g fat; 1.3g saturated fat; 10.1g carbohydrates; 8.7g sugars

Fat Burner Smoothie

Matcha green tea is not only packed with antioxidants but has been shown to help boost metabolism and weight loss. This thick shake is a great pick-me-up for a breakfast or before a workout. Using frozen banana and watermelon give this smoothie a deliciously thick, creamy texture. You don't have to buy a whole watermelon for this; simply buy little tubs of chopped prepared watermelon and freeze in advance. This is a very thick, almost pudding-like smoothie that is delicious eaten with a spoon. If you can't find matcha green tea powder, soak a couple of green tea bags in a little hot water overnight then add the liquid to the smoothie.

PREPARATION TIME: 5 minutes, plus freezing
SERVES 1

100g watermelon, chopped
1 small banana, chopped
1 tsp matcha green tea powder
1 tsp vanilla extract
250ml unsweetened almond milk
1 scoop (30g) vanilla protein powder

Place the watermelon and banana into the freezer and freeze for at least 4 hours (or overnight) until frozen.

Place the remaining ingredients in a blender and process briefly.
Add the frozen fruit and process again to form a thick smoothie.

*Per serving: 295 kcal; 27.8g protein; 5.2g fat, 0.2g saturated
fat; 39.6g carbohydrates; 27g sugars*

Breakfast Morning Pick-Me-Up

This will add a zing to your day! The orange provides plenty of vitamin C to keep your immune system healthy and energise the body, while the avocado provides healthy fats and gives this smoothie a delicious creamy texture. If you are making this for breakfast, add a scoop of protein powder.

PREPARATION TIME: 5 minutes
SERVES 1

1 orange, peeled and pips removed
¼ avocado, chopped
½ tsp grated fresh ginger
200ml coconut water
Pinch of cayenne pepper (optional)
1 scoop (30g) vanilla protein powder

Simply blend all the ingredients in a high-speed blender or Nutribullet until smooth.

Per serving: 248 kcal; 26.2g protein; 7.7g fat; 1.1g saturated fat; 23.4g carbohydrates; 14.1g sugars

Cinnamon Peanut Butter Shake

This indulgent shake is rich and satisfying – the oats provide additional fibre to help balance blood sugar and will keep you feeling fuller for longer.

PREPARATION TIME: 5 minutes
SERVES 1

2 tsp peanut butter
1 tsp ground cinnamon
1 small banana, chopped
1 tbsp gluten-free oats
1 scoop (30g) vanilla or chocolate protein powder
250ml unsweetened almond milk

Simply blend all the ingredients in a high-speed blender or Nutribullet until smooth.

Per serving: 381 kcal; 28.9g protein; 12.1g fat; 1.1g saturated fat; 43.9g carbohydrates; 20.6g sugars

Protein Chocolate Latte

This rich, creamy and indulgent 'latte' is an easy way to cram in a few more greens! The maca powder is optional but is great superfood that helps regulate stress hormones, which can interfere with our ability to lose weight.

PREPARATION TIME: 5 minutes
SERVES 1

Handful of spinach leaves
1 tbsp cocoa powder or raw cacao powder
1 scoop (30g) protein powder (vanilla or chocolate)
½ tsp ground cinnamon
1 tsp vanilla extract
1 tsp almond nut butter
1 tsp xylitol
250–300ml unsweetened almond milk

Simply blend together all the ingredients in a high-speed blender or Nutribullet until smooth.

Per serving: 257 kcal; 27.1g protein; 9.6g fat; 1.8g saturated fat; 22.6g carbohydrates; 4.7g sugars

RECILPES
Breakfasts

Overnight Bircher Protein Bowl

This is such an easy recipe and the variations are endless. You can add an extra teaspoon of tahini paste, which is a good source of healthy fats and calcium. You'll need to make this up the night before but it's great if you're short on time in the mornings as you can just make it up in a Tupperware container and take it to work with you the next day.

PREPARATION TIME: 10 minutes, plus soaking
SERVES 1

1 small banana
75ml unsweetened almond milk
1 tbsp raw cacao powder or 100% unsweetened cocoa
   powder
½ scoop (15g) vanilla or plain protein powder
1 tsp tahini paste
½ tsp ground cinnamon
15g pumpkin seeds
15g sunflower seeds
15g gluten-free oats

Place the banana, almond milk, cacao or cocoa powder, protein powder, tahini paste and cinnamon in a blender and process to form a thick cream.

Put the seeds and oats in the bottom of a bowl or Tupperware container and pour over the creamy banana and chocolate mixture. Stir well and then place in the fridge overnight to soak. This will keep in the fridge for 1–2 days.

Per serving: 471 kcal; 24.8g protein; 21.6g fat; 3.3g saturated fat; 46.7g carbohydrates; 18.5g sugars

Apple and Almond
Replace the tahini paste with almond nut butter and the banana with 100g apple sauce. Use vanilla protein powder and omit the cacao powder.

Fat Burner Matcha
Omit the cacao powder and cinnamon and use 1 teaspoon matcha green tea powder.

Strawberry and Coconut
Use coconut milk instead of almond milk and replace the banana with 100g strawberries.

Nutty Pear Granola Clusters

This nut-based granola is naturally sweetened with pear and is packed with healthy fats and protein to keep you feeling energised throughout the morning. Serve this with a dollop of coconut yoghurt and a handful of fresh berries. On its own, the granola makes a fabulously healthy on-the-go snack too. Make up a batch and store in an airtight container.

PREPARATION TIME: 15 minutes
COOKING TIME: 50 minutes
MAKES 16 servings

115g gluten-free oats (or use quinoa, millet or buckwheat flakes)
60g flaked almonds
60g walnut pieces
2 tbsp chia seeds
30g shelled hemp seed
60g sunflower seeds
60g pumpkin seeds
60g sesame seeds
30g coconut oil, melted
1 scoop (30g) plain or vanilla protein powder
1 ripe pear, chopped
1 tbsp ground cinnamon

4–6 tbsp apple juice or coconut water
60g goji berries or other dried berries

Preheat the oven to 180°C/fan 160°C/gas mark 4 and line a baking tray with baking parchment.

Put the oats (or flakes), nuts and seeds in a bowl and mix thoroughly. Put the coconut oil, protein powder (if using), chopped pear and cinnamon into a blender and process until smooth. Add enough apple juice or coconut water to form a smooth, thick paste. Pour the wet mixture over the oats, and combine thoroughly with your hands to ensure the oats and nuts are well coated.

Spread the mixture on to the lined baking tray and bake for 30–40 minutes until golden and crisp. Allow the granola to cool, then stir in the dried berries. Store in an airtight container for up to 2 weeks.

Per 50g serving: 205 kcal; 7.1g protein; 14.6g fat; 3.1g saturated fat; 11.8g carbohydrates; 4.7g sugars

Grab-and-Go Vanilla and Chocolate Chip Protein Bars

These simple, no-cook protein bars are perfect for a breakfast on the go or healthy snack. I like to use xylitol to keep the sugar content low. Keep these in the freezer as they taste great semi-frozen too.

PREPARATION TIME: 15 minutes, plus chilling
MAKES 8 bars

50g coconut oil
60g nut or seed butter or tahini paste
1 tbsp vanilla extract
8 tbsp unsweetened almond milk
50g xylitol
100g coconut flour
100g vanilla protein powder
60g sugar-free and dairy-free chocolate chips
30g desiccated coconut

Line a 20cm square baking tin with greased baking parchment and set aside.

Place the coconut oil, nut butter, vanilla, almond milk and xylitol in a pan and place over a low heat until melted. Stir well to combine.

Put the coconut flour and protein powder in a food processor, pulse briefly to combine and then pour in the wet ingredients. Process to form a crumbly mixture, then add the chocolate chips and coconut and pulse briefly to combine.

Transfer the mixture to the prepared tin and press in firmly. Place in the fridge to chill for at least 30 minutes.

Per bar: 286 kcal; 14g protein; 18.6g fat; 11.9g saturated fat; 20.7g carbohydrates; 2.2g sugars

Vanilla Waffles with Peaches

This recipe produces delicious, crispy waffles that are delicious hot or cold. I use almond flour as it is higher in protein and lower in carbs than regular flour. The protein powder is optional; if you omit it use a little less almond milk. You can top these with any fresh or poached fruit, depending on what is in season.

PREPARATION TIME: 10 minutes
COOKING TIME: 5–10 minutes
MAKES 2 large waffles

60g almond flour
1 scoop (30g) plain or vanilla protein powder (optional)
1 tbsp vanilla extract
Pinch of salt
1 tbsp ground flaxseed
2 tsp baking powder
100ml unsweetened almond milk
1 tbsp melted coconut oil or olive oil
2 tbsp xylitol or 1 tsp granulated stevia, to taste

To serve
2 peaches, stoned and thinly sliced
Juice of 1 orange

Preheat and grease a waffle maker.

Place all the ingredients in a food processor or blender and process to form a thick batter. Allow the mixture to sit for 5 minutes and then blend again.

Pour the batter into the waffle maker and cook for 5–6 minutes (or follow the manufacturer's instructions).

Meanwhile place the sliced peaches in a small pan with the orange juice and simmer over a low heat for a couple of minutes until softened. Serve with the waffles.

Per waffle (with peaches): 406 kcal; 20.3g protein; 26g fat; 2.3g saturated fat; 30.6g carbohydrates; 11.5g sugars

Millet and Apricot Porridge

Creamy and comforting, this is a fabulous porridge you can prepare the day before and reheat in the morning if you are rushed for time. If apricots are not in season use 1 pear or apple instead. For additional protein stir in a spoonful of protein powder into your cooked porridge.

PREPARATION TIME: 10 minutes
COOKING TIME: 25 minutes
SERVES 4

200g millet
750ml water
4 fresh apricots, stoned and chopped
150ml unsweetened almond milk
2 tsp cashew nut butter
1 tsp xylitol
1 tsp ground cinnamon
2 tsp ground flaxseed
30g/1 scoop protein powder

Put the millet and water in a pan and bring to the boil. Reduce the heat and simmer, covered, for 15 minutes.

Add the fresh apricots and continue to cook for a further 10 minutes until all the water has been absorbed. Set aside.

Put the remaining ingredients into a blender or Nutribullet and process until smooth. Pour the creamy mixture into the millet porridge and stir well. Serve hot or cold.

Per serving: 140 kcal; 9.7g protein; 3.5g fat; 0.4g saturated fat; 16.6g carbohydrates; 2.8g sugars

Grilled Grapefruit

This makes a delicious, refreshing snack or light breakfast. Instead of smothering it with sugar or syrup, use pink grapefruit, which is naturally much sweeter – you can always add a little xylitol or granulated stevia if needed. Top with a spoonful of nut cream or yoghurt.

PREPARATION TIME: 5 minutes
COOKING TIME: 5–6 minutes
SERVES 2

1 pink grapefruit
½ tsp ground cinnamon
2 tsp xylitol or granulated stevia (optional)
1 tbsp nut cream or coconut yoghurt, to serve

Preheat your grill to high.

Cut the grapefruit in half and place on a baking tray. Sprinkle with the cinnamon and xylitol or stevia, if using. Grill the grapefruit under the hot grill until golden, about 5–6 minutes. Serve topped with the nut cream or yoghurt.

Per serving: 37 kcal; 0.7g protein; 0.2g fat; 0g saturated fat; 9.7g carbohydrates; 5.9g sugars

Coconut Yoghurt with Berry Jam

This makes a simple breakfast or healthy snack any time of day. Using chia seeds to make the jam adds plenty of Omega-3 fats and fibre too. If fresh berries aren't in season you can use a bag of frozen mixed berries or cherries instead. Top this with some mixed seeds or a handful of Nutty Pear Granola Clusters (see page 103) for a more substantial dish.

PREPARATION TIME: 5 minutes, plus chilling
COOKING TIME: 5 minutes
SERVES 2

250g coconut yoghurt, shop-bought or homemade (see page 81)
1 tbsp desiccated coconut, to serve

For the berry jam
125g strawberries, chopped
125g frozen pitted cherries
1 tbsp lemon juice
1 tbsp xylitol
3 tbsp chia seeds

First make the jam. Place the strawberries and cherries in a small pan with the lemon juice. Warm gently for about 5 minutes, covered. Remove the lid and mash up the fruit with a wooden spoon.

Add the xylitol and chia seeds and stir well for a minute. Take off the heat and beat well. Pour into a jar and place in the fridge to chill – it will take about 20–30 minutes to firm up (the jam will keep in the fridge for 3–4 days and can also be frozen for up to 1 month).

Divide the coconut yoghurt between two bowls and stir in the jam. Sprinkle with a little desiccated coconut to serve, if liked.

Per serving: 200 kcal; 5.1g protein; 7.5g fat; 0.9g saturated fat; 31.8g carbohydrates; 16.3g sugars

Chia Layered Puddings

Chia puddings are so simple to prepare and make the perfect slimming breakfast. Chia seeds are packed with fibre to keep blood sugar levels stable through the morning. Put together this parfait in the evening, pop it in the fridge overnight, and enjoy a healthy breakfast the next day. For ease I use a tin of mandarin segments in natural juice.

PREPARATION TIME: 10 minutes, plus overnight soaking
SERVES 2

1 x 250g tin mandarin segments in natural juice
5 tbsp (50g) chia seeds
150ml coconut milk or unsweetened almond milk
1 scoop (30g) plain or vanilla protein powder
100g coconut yoghurt, shop-bought or homemade (see page 81)

Drain the mandarin segments, reserving the juice and place them in a bowl. Chill until needed.

Place the chia seeds in a jug with the coconut or almond milk. Add enough of the reserved mandarin juice to make 300ml and stir in the protein powder, if using. Stir well and leave to soak in the fridge overnight.

The next morning place a little of the chia pudding in the bottom of two glasses. Add a few mandarin segments followed by the remaining chia pudding. Finish with a few more mandarin segments and top with the coconut yoghurt.

Per serving: 266 kcal; 16.9g protein; 9.3g fat; 1g saturated fat; 32.8g carbohydrates; 21.6g sugars

Coconut Quinoa bowl with Blueberries

A deliciously warming breakfast option. The addition of tahini creates a wonderful creamy texture as well as providing plenty of calcium, zinc and a dose of healthy fats. If you want to boost the portein further, stir in a spoonful of protein powder at the end of cooking. Quinoa is a fabulous vegan pseudo grain that is rich in amino acids. Quinoa can be bitter if it isn't rinsed really well so if you have time soak in water the night before then rinse before using. You can also make this porridge the day before and keep in the fridge – simply reheat in a pan with a little water added.

PREPARATION TIME: 10 minutes
COOKING TIME: 20 minutes
SERVES 2

90g quinoa, ideally soaked in cold water overnight
150ml water
150ml coconut milk
1 tsp granulated stevia (optional)
1 tsp tahini paste
1 tbsp protein powder (optional)

For the blueberry compote
200g fresh or frozen blueberries

2 tbsp water
1 tsp xylitol, or to taste
2 tsp cornflour

First make the compote. Place the berries, water and xylitol in a pan, cover and simmer over a low heat for 2–3 minutes to soften. Mix together the cornflour with 2 tablespoons water to form a smooth paste. Add this to the pan and stir for 1–2 minutes until the mixture thickens. Set aside to cool (this can be made ahead of time and kept in the fridge until needed).

Rinse the (soaked) quinoa well in a sieve and then place in a pan with the water, coconut milk and stevia, if using. Bring to the boil then simmer over a very low heat for 15 minutes until the grain is soft and most of the liquid absorbed. Stir in the tahini. Spoon the porridge into bowls and top with the berry compote

Per serving: 218 kcal; 8.3g protein; 4.3g fat; 0.7g saturated fat; 37.3g carbohydrates; 10.5g sugars

Apple and Raspberry Breakfast Crisp

Crumble for breakfast? With this nutritious option the answer is yes! It's also delicious enough to serve as a pudding or snack. Using almonds for the crumble topping increases the protein content to keep you feeling energised and using frozen raspberries makes this an easy recipe to throw together. You may wish to combine this dish with a protein shake or add protein powder to the topping in order to get additional protein in the morning.

PREPARATION TIME: 10 minutes
COOKING TIME: 30–40 minutes
SERVES 6

3 eating apples, cored and thinly sliced
200g frozen raspberries
150g ground almonds
1 tbsp protein powder (optional)
1 tsp ground cinnamon
30g xylitol
1 tbsp vanilla extract
60g coconut oil, melted
Soya or coconut yoghurt (see page 11) to serve (optional)

Preheat the oven to 180°C/fan 160°C/gas mark 4.

Place the apples and raspberries in the bottom of a baking dish. In a bowl mix together the ground almonds, cinnamon, xylitol, vanilla and coconut oil. Scatter the almond mixture over the top of the fruit and bake in the oven for 30–40 minutes until golden and bubbling.

Serve with soya or coconut yoghurt, if wished.

Per serving: 279 kcal; 5.9g protein; 24.1g fat; 9.8g saturated fat; 11.7g carbohydrates; 6.2g sugars

Protein Banana Pancakes

These pancakes are so simple to make and are a great way to use up over-ripe bananas. They taste fabulous topped with a little coconut yoghurt or cream and fresh berries, and the addition of aquafaba (the liquid from the can of cooked chickpeas) also gives it a really light texture. If you don't have protein powder you can replace it with some ground almonds instead.

PREPARATION TIME: 10 minutes
COOKING TIME: 6 minutes
SERVES 2

100g gluten-free oats or quinoa flakes
1 scoop (30g) plain or vanilla protein powder
200ml unsweetened almond milk or coconut milk
3 tbsp aquafaba (optional)
2 tsp baking powder
Pinch of salt
1 ripe banana, roughly chopped
Coconut oil, for frying
Coconut yoghurt (see page 81) and fresh berries, to serve

Place the oats or quinoa flakes in a food processor or blender and blitz until you have a fine flour. Add the remaining ingredients and process to form a thick, smooth batter. Pour into a measuring jug.

Melt a little coconut oil in a frying pan over a medium heat. Drop spoonfuls of the batter into the pan to make little blinis (you may need to cook these in several batches, depending on the size of your pan). Cook for 2 minutes or until the edges start to turn golden. Flip over and cook for a further minute. Continue until all the batter is used up.

Serve with a dollop of coconut yoghurt and some fresh berries.

Per serving (without yoghurt and berries): 325 kcal; 17.8g protein; 7.7g fat; 1.3g saturated fat; 47.9g carbohydrates; 10.1g sugars

Tofu Vegetable Scramble

If you miss scrambled eggs at breakfast then do give this vegan alternative a try. When tofu is crumbled and flavoured with spices it makes a healthy, protein-rich replacement. Serve with slices of avocado for a filling and energising dish.

PREPARATION TIME: 10 minutes
COOKING TIME: 8 minutes
SERVES 2

1 tsp coconut oil
2 spring onions, chopped
1 garlic clove, crushed
6 mushrooms, sliced
½ red pepper, finely chopped
250g firm tofu, drained
Pinch of smoked paprika
Pinch of ground turmeric
1 tbsp nutritional yeast flakes
1 tsp tamari soy sauce
1 tomato, chopped
150g baby spinach leaves
Sea salt and black pepper

Heat the oil in a frying pan over a medium heat and add the spring onions, garlic, mushrooms and red pepper. Sauté gently for 2–3 minutes until the pepper has softened.

Crumble over the tofu and stir into the vegetables with the spices, yeast flakes and soy sauce. Season to taste with salt and pepper. Cook, stirring, for 3–4 minutes until the tofu begins to turn golden. Add the tomato and spinach leaves and stir for a minute until the spinach has wilted.

Spoon onto two plates and serve immediately.

Per serving: 165 kcal; 16.1g protein; 8.1g fat; 2.1g saturated fat; 7.1g carbohydrates; 4.3g sugars

Vegan Seeded Bread

This gluten-free bread is so easy to make – as long as you remember to soak the quinoa the night before! It's high in protein, thanks to the quinoa and seeds. This is best served on the day it is made but can also be sliced and frozen too. Top with coconut oil or nut butter or serve alongside the Tofu Vegetable Scramble (see page 122).

PREPARATION TIME: 10 minutes, plus overnight soaking
COOKING TIME: 50 minutes
MAKES 1 loaf (10 slices)

50g quinoa, soaked in cold water overnight
50g ground pumpkin seeds
50g ground flaxseed
30g coconut flour
50g chia seeds
1 tsp bicarbonate of soda
½ tsp xanthan gum
300ml water
1 tbsp olive oil
1 tbsp psyllium husks
½ tsp sea salt
1 tbsp lemon juice
1 tsp xylitol
50g mixed seeds

Preheat the oven to 160°C/fan 140°C/gas mark 3 and grease and line a 900g loaf tin with baking parchment.

Drain and rinse the soaked quinoa and place in a food processor with the ground pumpkin seeds, ground flaxseed, coconut flour and chia seeds and process to combine. Add the remaining ingredients except the mixed seeds and process until the mixture is almost smooth. Stir in the mixed seeds, reserving a few for the top.

Pour the mixture into the prepared loaf tin and scatter the remaining seeds on top. Bake in the oven for 50 minutes until a skewer or sharp knife inserted into the loaf comes out clean. Turn out onto a wire rack and allow to cool before slicing.

Per slice: 143 kcal; 5g protein; 9g fat; 1.5g saturated fat; 10.2g carbohydrates; 0.6g sugars

Veggie Fritters with Yoghurt Herb Sauce

These delicious fritters are light and crispy and make a fabulous light lunch or breakfast option. Using chickpeas and chickpea (gram) flour is a great way to increase the protein content, as well as helping to bind the mixture together. This recipe uses half a 400g tin of chickpeas or butterbeans so you may wish to double the recipe and store the rest in the fridge and use as a snack or for lunch the following day. The yoghurt sauce will keep in the fridge for 3–4 days.

PREPARATION TIME: 10 minutes
COOKING TIME: 10 minutes
MAKES 6 fritters (to serve 2)

110g tinned chickpeas or butterbeans, rinsed and drained
1 courgette (150g), grated
30g chickpea (gram) flour
1 tsp olive oil
½ tsp ground cumin
1 tbsp nutritional yeast flakes
¼ red onion, finely chopped
1 tbsp chopped fresh coriander leaves
Sea salt and black pepper
Coconut oil, for frying

For the yoghurt sauce

100g coconut yoghurt, shop-bought or homemade (see page 81)

1 tsp chopped fresh coriander leaves

1 tsp chopped fresh mint leaves

1 tsp chopped fresh parsley

Sea salt and black pepper

For the yoghurt sauce simply mix all the ingredients together and store in the fridge until needed. This will keep in the fridge for 2–3 days.

Place the chickpeas or butterbeans in a bowl and mash roughly with the back of a fork. Add the remaining ingredients and combine together well; taste and adjust the seasoning.

Heat the coconut oil in a frying pan. Working in batches, drop 2–3 spoonfuls of the batter into the pan and press down lightly to form little round fritters. Cook for 3 minutes until the edges start to turn golden, then flip over and cook for a further 2 minutes until cooked through. Serve with the herb yoghurt.

Per serving: 162 kcal; 10.3g protein; 5g fat; 1.8g saturated fat; 19.5g carbohydrates; 5.1g sugars

RECIPES
Soups

Roasted Pumpkin, Butterbean and Apple Soup

Roasting pumpkin produces a rich, sweet, caramel flavour and when blended with butterbeans creates a wonderfully creamy, thick soup. If you are short of time then make use of bags of frozen chunks of pumpkin – saving you chopping and peeling time. Adding the apple gives the soup a lovely sweetness as well as providing soluble fibre to support blood sugar levels. You can use butternut squash instead of pumpkin if wished. This freezes well (up to 3 months) or will keep in the fridge for 3–4 days.

PREPARATION TIME: 15 minutes
COOKING TIME: 55 minutes
SERVES 4

600g (prepared weight) pumpkin or butternut squash (or use fresh or frozen ready prepared chunks)
2 tsp olive oil
1 tbsp coconut oil or olive oil
1 red onion, chopped
1 carrot, chopped
2 garlic cloves, crushed
½ tsp ground cinnamon
½ tsp ground cumin
600ml vegetable stock
1 apple, cored and chopped

2 x 400g tin butterbeans, rinsed and drained
Sea salt and black pepper

For the topping
30g pumpkin seeds
Olive oil, for drizzling
Large pinch of ground cumin
Sea salt

Preheat the oven to 190°C/fan 170°C/gas mark 5.

If using a fresh pumpkin cut the pumpkin into wedges, reserving the seeds for the topping. Cut the wedges into 3cm cubes. Place the pumpkin on a baking tray, drizzle with the olive oil and season with salt and pepper. Bake in the oven for 40 minutes until soft, golden and caramelised. Leave to cool slightly then peel off the skins with your hands and discard. Set the roasted pumpkin aside and reduce the oven temperature to 180°C/fan 160°C/gas mark 4.

Meanwhile prepare the topping. If using a fresh pumpkin rinse the reserved seeds and then rub dry with a tea towel. Spread the seeds out on a baking tray and drizzle with a little olive oil. Sprinkle with sea salt and cumin and mix well to coat. Bake in the oven for 10 minutes until lightly golden. Allow to cool.

Heat the coconut oil in a large pan over a medium heat and add the onion, carrot, garlic and spices. Sauté gently for 5 minutes then pour over the stock. Add the pumpkin, apple and butterbeans and simmer for 10 minutes until the apple is soft.

Using a food processor, blender or hand-held stick blender, purée the soup until thick and creamy. Ladle the soup into bowls then top with the spicy toasted pumpkin seeds.

Per serving: 293 kcal; 11.5g protein; 9.3g fat; 3g saturated fat; 34.4g carbohydrates; 14.4g sugars

Ramen Tofu Noodle Bowl

This is such a light, refreshing soup and low-carb too, thanks to the addition of vegetable noodles. You could also use kelp noodles, which are available online – they are a good source of iodine, which is important for healthy thyroid function, metabolism and weight loss.

PREPARATION TIME: 10 minutes
COOKING TIME: 14 minutes
SERVES 4

1 medium courgette (or use 150g kelp noodles, soaked and
    roughly chopped)
1 tbsp coconut oil
450g firm tofu, drained and cut into 2cm cubes
2 spring onions, finely chopped
2 garlic cloves, crushed
600ml vegetable stock
2 pak choi, roughly chopped
150g shiitake mushrooms, sliced
1 tbsp white miso paste
2 tbsp tamari soy sauce
Handful of beansprouts

To serve
1 tbsp toasted sesame seeds
1 tbsp chopped coriander leaves

Use a spiraliser to make long noodles from the courgette; alternatively use a swivel potato peeler to create long strips. Set aside.

Heat 2 teaspoons of the coconut oil in a frying pan and add the tofu. Sauté for 5 minutes over a medium-high heat until the tofu is lightly golden. Remove from the pan and set aside.

Heat the remaining coconut oil in a pan and sauté the spring onion and garlic for 1–2 minutes over a medium heat. Pour in the vegetable stock and bring to the boil. Add the pak choi and mushrooms and simmer for 5 minutes until the pak choi has wilted. Stir in the miso paste, tamari, beansprouts, tofu and courgette (or kelp) noodles and stir briefly. Turn off the heat and allow the soup to sit for 1–2 minutes to allow the noodles to soften.

Ladle the soup into bowls and scatter over the sesame seeds and coriander to serve.

Per serving: 176 kcal; 14.5g protein; 10.6g fat; 3g saturated fat; 5.4g carbohydrates; 3.7g sugars

Broccoli Coconut Cream Soup

This thick and creamy soup makes an ideal slimming lunch. It actually uses a couple of tins of cannellini beans to really boost the protein content. You could also make up a bigger batch and keep it in the freezer or fridge ready for a healthy snack too.

PREPARATION TIME: 10 minutes
COOKING TIME: 12 minutes
SERVES 4

1 tsp olive oil or coconut oil
2 garlic cloves, crushed
½ tsp ground cumin
300ml vegetable stock
1 x 400ml tin coconut milk
1 head of broccoli (250g), broken into florets
100g spinach leaves
2 x 400g tins cannellini beans, rinsed and drained
1 tbsp lemon juice
1 tbsp chopped fresh parsley
2 tbsp nutritional yeast flakes (optional)
Sea salt and black pepper

Heat the coconut oil in a medium pan and add the garlic and cumin. Sauté over a medium heat for 1 minute.

Add the stock, coconut milk and broccoli and cook for 10 minutes. Stir in the spinach, cannellini beans, lemon juice, parsley and nutritional yeast flakes, if using. Let the spinach wilt for a minute.

Using a food processor, blender or hand-held stick blender, process the soup until smooth. Taste and adjust the seasoning, then spoon into bowls and serve.

Per serving: 163 kcal; 12.7g protein; 2.7g fat; 0.6g saturated fat; 22.1g carbohydrates; 7.3g sugars

Spiced Lentil Soup

Lentils are a great source of protein for vegans, and provide plenty of energising iron too. This is a thick, chunky soup that is wonderfully comforting, making it a filling lunch option. If preferred you can purée the soup for a smoother texture.

PREPARATION TIME: 15 minutes
COOKING TIME: 45 minutes
SERVES 2

1 tbsp coconut oil
½ tsp cumin seeds
1 garlic clove, crushed
1 small red onion, finely chopped
1 carrot, diced
1 celery stick, finely chopped
½ tsp grated fresh ginger
½ tsp ground cumin
1 cinnamon stick
1 tbsp tomato purée
625ml vegetable stock
100g split red lentils
Large handful of spinach leaves
1 tbsp pomegranate molasses or lemon juice
1 tbsp chopped fresh mint leaves
1 tbsp chopped fresh coriander leaves

Sea salt and black pepper
2 tbsp coconut yoghurt, to serve (optional)

Heat the oil in a large pan over a medium heat. Add the cumin seeds, garlic, onion, celery and carrot and sauté for about 10 minutes until soft.

Stir in the ginger, ground cumin and cinnamon stick and sauté for a minute before adding the tomato purée and stock. Stir in the lentils and cook, covered, over a low-medium heat for about 30 minutes until the lentils are very soft.

Remove the pan from the heat and stir in the spinach leaves to let them wilt. Remove the cinnamon stick and then, using a potato masher, break up the lentils lightly. Stir in the pomegranate molasses or lemon juice and fresh herbs and taste and adjust the seasoning. Divide the soup between two bowls and top each with a tablespoon of coconut yoghurt, if using.

Per serving: 284 kcal; 13.8g protein; 6.1g fat; 4.1g saturated fat; 40.1g carbohydrates; 12g sugars

Roasted Tomato and Red Pepper Soup

A simple, refreshing summer soup. There's little preparation involved – just chop up the tomatoes and peppers and roast until golden. Blending in the tin of beans provides protein and fibre and makes the soup deliciously creamy. This could also be served cold.

PREPARATION TIME: 10 minutes
COOKING TIME: 20 minutes
SERVES 2

2 red peppers
4 plum tomatoes
1 small red onion
2 garlic cloves
1 tbsp olive oil
Pinch of smoked paprika
500ml vegetable stock
2 sun-dried tomatoes in oil, drained
1 x 400g tin cannellini or butterbeans, rinsed and drained
1 tbsp finely chopped fresh basil
Sea salt and black pepper

Preheat the oven to 200°C/fan 180°C/gas mark 6.

Cut the peppers into large chunks, discarding the core and seeds. Cut the tomatoes and red onion into quarters. Put all the vegetables and whole garlic cloves on a baking tray, drizzle over the olive oil and toss gently. Season with salt and pepper and roast in the oven for 20 minutes until the vegetables are soft and lightly golden.

Tip all the vegetables into a food processor or a blender with the paprika, stock, sun-dried tomatoes and drained beans. Process until smooth and creamy.

Pour into a pan and place over a low–medium heat until heated through. Taste and adjust the seasoning and then stir in the chopped basil. Ladle into bowls to serve.

Per serving: 229 kcal; 9.9g protein; 8.7g fat; 1.4g saturated fat; 27.5g carbohydrates; 12.7g sugars

Creamy Sweetcorn and Cauliflower Chowder

Sweetcorn is high in fibre and contains a reasonable amount of protein, making it a useful addition to vegan dishes. Roasting the cauliflower really brings out its creamy flavour.

PREPARATION TIME: 10 minutes
COOKING TIME: 40 minutes
SERVES 2

½ head of cauliflower (250g), cut into small florets
1 tbsp olive oil
1 garlic clove, crushed
½ tsp ground cumin
1 tsp coconut oil
½ onion, finely chopped
1 celery stick, finely chopped
1 tsp caraway seeds
¼ tsp smoked paprika
500ml vegetable stock
150g tinned sweetcorn, drained
1 tbsp chopped chives
1 tsp lemon zest
Salt and white pepper

Preheat the oven to 180°C/fan 160°C/gas mark 4.

Toss the cauliflower florets with the olive oil, garlic and cumin in a bowl and then spread out on a baking tray. Roast for 30 minutes until golden.

Melt the coconut oil in a large pan over a medium heat and add the onion, celery, caraway seeds and paprika; sauté for 5 minutes until soft. Add the vegetable stock, sweetcorn and roasted cauliflower. Season with salt and white pepper and simmer for 5 minutes.

Transfer half of the soup to a food processor or blender and process until smooth. Return to the pan, along with the chopped chives and lemon zest. Stir until warmed through and then ladle into bowls to serve.

Per serving: 129 kcal; 7.6g protein; 8.2g fat; 2.2g saturated fat; 6.8g carbohydrates; 5g sugars

Green Energy Soup

Light and refreshing, this is a simple soup to prepare and perfect for when time is short. Adding cashew nuts to the soup creates a wonderful creamy texture and provides protein and healthy fats too.

PREPARATION TIME: 10 minutes
COOKING TIME: 7 minutes
SERVES 4

500ml vegetable stock
½ onion, finely chopped
200g frozen peas
200g spinach or kale, chopped
50g cashew nuts
1 garlic clove, crushed
1 tbsp apple cider vinegar
2 tsp tamari soy sauce
1 tbsp chopped fresh mint leaves
1 tbsp chopped fresh parsley
Sea salt and black pepper
Soya yoghurt or coconut yoghurt (see page 81), to serve
   (optional)

Bring the stock to the boil. Add the onion, peas, spinach or kale, cashew nuts and garlic and cook for 6–7 minutes until the peas are soft.

Transfer to a blender or food processor (or use a hand-held stick blender) along with the remaining ingredients and process until smooth. Taste and adjust the seasoning and then ladle into bowls to serve. Top with a dollop of yoghurt, if liked.

Per serving: 125 kcal: 6.9g protein; 7.1g fat; 1.3g saturated fat; 8.2g carbohydrates; 3.1g sugars

Salads and Light Dishes

Creamy Caesar-style Kale Salad

This is a power-packed salad. Kale is a surprisingly good source of protein, which together with the seeds and nuts makes this a satisfying and energising dish. The salad will keep well in the fridge for a couple of days.

PREPARATION TIME: 10 minutes, plus soaking
SERVES 2

200g kale, leaves torn from stems and chopped
200g cherry tomatoes, halved
4 celery sticks, finely chopped
1 apple, cored and diced
2 tbsp shelled hemp seeds or toasted mixed seeds
Sea salt and black pepper

For the dressing
70g cashew nuts, soaked in water for 20 minutes then
    drained
1 garlic clove
½ tsp Dijon mustard
½ tsp onion salt
1 tsp xylitol
2 tbsp nutritional yeast flakes
1 tbsp tamari soy sauce
1 tbsp apple cider vinegar

2 tbsp lemon juice
2–3 tbsp water
Pinch of black pepper

First make the dressing. Blend all the ingredients in a high-speed blender with just enough water to make a thick and creamy consistency.

Place the kale in a large bowl and pour over the dressing. Start to massage the kale with your hands until it wilts and softens and takes on a 'cooked' texture. Add the tomatoes, celery, apple and hemp seeds to the bowl and mix gently. Season to taste and then divide between two bowls to serve.

Per serving: 395 kcal; 19.9g protein; 26.1g fat; 4.1g saturated fat; 20.5g carbohydrates; 10.8g sugars

Harissa Roasted Vegetable Salad with Nut Cheese

This warming, comforting salad is perfect for the winter months and is delicious served hot or cold. Use a pouch of ready-cooked lentils will save you time too.

PREPARATION TIME: 15 minutes
COOKING TIME: 40 minutes
SERVES 4

1 medium sweet potato (250g), peeled and cut into 1cm chunks
1 red pepper, cut into large chunks
500g celeriac, cut into 1cm chunks
1 medium carrot, thickly sliced
1 red onion, cut into wedges
1 tbsp olive oil
1 tbsp balsamic vinegar
400g cooked puy lentils, drained
200g bag of mixed salad leaves
60g Vegan Nut Cheese (see page 87)
Sea salt and black pepper
Handful of chopped fresh parsley, to serve

For the harissa dressing
2 tsp harissa paste

1 tsp ground cumin
Juice of 1 lemon
2 tsp xylitol
2 tsp olive oil
Sea salt and black pepper

Preheat the oven to 200°C/fan 180°C/gas mark 6.

Arrange the vegetables and onion on a baking tray and drizzle with the oil and vinegar. Season with salt and pepper and roast in the oven for 40 minutes until tender and lightly golden. Ten minutes before the end of the cooking time add the lentils and toss through the vegetables.

Whisk together all the dressing ingredients, adding a splash of water if needed to combine.

Place the salad greens on a platter and top with the roasted vegetables and lentils. Add dollops of the cheese on top. Pour the dressing over the top and scatter with parsley to serve.

Per serving: 319 kcal; 14.1g protein; 11.2g fat; 1.7g saturated fat; 40g carbohydrates; 11.6g sugars

Vietnamese Tofu/Tempeh Salad

This Asian salad is packed with flavour and crunch. The tangy lime dressing keeps it light and refreshing while the tofu provides plenty of protein to keep you energised.

PREPARATION TIME: 15 minutes
COOKING TIME: 6 minutes
SERVES 4

2 tsp coconut oil
600g firm tofu or tempeh (defrosted), drained and cut into 2cm cubes
2 carrots, cut into julienne or spiralised
1 medium courgette, cut into julienne or spiralised
1 red pepper, thinly sliced
1 cucumber, halved lengthways, deseeded and thinly sliced
2 spring onions, finely chopped
½ red chilli, deseeded and diced
Handful of baby spinach leaves
Handful of fresh mint leaves, chopped
Small handful of fresh coriander, chopped

For the dressing
1 garlic clove, crushed
1/2 red chilli, deseeded and chopped
1 tsp grated fresh ginger

125ml lime juice (from about 4 limes)
1 tbsp tamari soy sauce
1 tbsp xylitol or granulated stevia

Heat the coconut oil in a frying pan and add the tofu. Fry all over for 5–6 minutes until the tofu is lightly golden. Drain on kitchen paper and set aside

Whisk all the dressing ingredients together in a bowl until combined.

Place all the vegetables and herbs in a large bowl and top with the fried tofu cubes. Drizzle over the dressing and serve immediately.

Per serving: 192 kcal; 14.7g protein; 8g fat; 2.2g saturated fat; 11.6g carbohydrates; 8.1g sugars

Middle Eastern Chickpea Salad

A delicious, simple salad full of Middle Eastern flavours. The lemon pomegranate dressing can be made ahead of time and kept in a screw-topped jar for 2–3 days – it's wonderful drizzled over steamed vegetables and cooked quinoa too. Try replacing the tinned chickpeas with Spiced Crunchy Chickpeas (see page 245).

PREPARATION TIME: 15 minutes
SERVES 4

3 x 400g tins chickpeas, rinsed and drained
1 cucumber, finely diced
1 red onion, diced
1 red chilli, deseeded and diced
4 radishes, thinly sliced
1 red pepper, thinly sliced
200g cherry tomatoes, halved
1 romaine lettuce, shredded
Handful of freshly chopped mint
Handful of freshly chopped coriander
Handful of freshly chopped parsley
Sea salt and black pepper

For the lemon pomegranate dressing
4 tbsp pomegranate molasses

Zest and juice of 1 lemon
1 garlic clove, crushed
1 tsp ground cumin
2 tsp xylitol or granulated stevia
1 tbsp olive oil, flaxseed oil or Omega-blend oil

Place all the dressing ingredients in a screw-topped jar and shake until well combined.

Place the chickpeas into a large serving bowl and add all the remaining salad ingredients. Drizzle over the dressing and toss lightly before serving.

Per serving: 331 kcal; 14.3g protein; 8.1g fat; 0.9g saturated fat; 44.6g carbohydrates; 14.1g sugars

Warm Lentil, Tomato and Olive Salad with Tahini Dressing

A fabulous, speedy protein salad, which can be served warm or cold. The tahini cream is also wonderful drizzled over cooked vegetables or used to top the Tex Mex Burgers (see page 187). Tahini is rich in minerals such as phosphorus, lecithin, magnesium, potassium and iron and is a great source of protein and healthy fats. If time is short use a couple of tins (or pouches) of cooked lentils.

PREPARATION TIME: 15 minutes
COOKING TIME: 17 minutes
SERVES 4

250g puy lentils, rinsed
1 tsp coconut oil
200g cherry tomatoes, halved
2 garlic cloves, crushed
4 celery sticks, finely chopped
1 small red onion, finely chopped
100g black olives, drained and halved
Handful of chopped fresh parsley

For the dressing
2 tbsp tahini paste
Juice of 1 lemon

1 tbsp apple cider vinegar
2 tsp xylitol or granulated stevia
½ tsp ground cumin
Sea salt and black pepper

Place the lentils in a pan and cover with water. Bring to the boil and simmer for 20 minutes until cooked. Drain and set aside. Melt the coconut oil in a frying pan over a medium heat. Add the cherry tomatoes, garlic, celery and onion and sauté gently for 3–4 minutes, just to soften the tomatoes. Stir in the lentils and olives and heat through.

To make the dressing whisk all the ingredients together (or shake in a screw-topped jar) until combined; taste and adjust the seasoning. Add about 2 tablespoons of water to make a thick dressing. Pour the dressing over the lentils in the pan and stir until warmed through.

Spoon the salad onto plates and scatter with chopped parsley to serve.

Per serving: 288 kcal; 17.8g protein; 9.5g fat; 1.9g saturated fat; 33.6g carbohydrates; 3.5g sugars

Roasted Beetroot and Carrot Salad with Hazelnut Dressing

Roasting beetroot is the best way to bring out its natural sweetness and, with the toasted nuts, makes a delicious, filling salad. If you can't find hazelnut oil then use walnut or flaxseed oil instead. The cooked tofu pieces provide additional protein but you can replace with a couple of tins of cooked mixed beans for a soy-free option.

PREPARATION TIME: 10 minutes
COOKING TIME: 50 minutes
SERVES 4

4 small beetroots, wiped clean and cut in half
300g baby carrots
2 leeks, cut into 2cm slices
1 red onion, cut into wedges
1 garlic clove
Sprig of fresh thyme
1 tbsp olive oil
2 handfuls of rocket or watercress
600g cooked tofu pieces (see Vietnamese Tofu Salad, page 153, or buy pre-cooked marinated tofu)
60g toasted hazelnuts, roughly chopped
Sea salt and black pepper

For the dressing
3 tbsp hazelnut oil
1 tsp xylitol
1 tbsp red wine vinegar
1/2 tsp Dijon mustard

Preheat the oven to 200°C/fan 180°C/gas mark 6.

Place a large piece of foil on a baking tray. Place the beetroot, carrot, leeks, onion and whole garlic clove on the foil. Run your fingers down the thyme sprig to release the thyme leaves and scatter over the vegetables. Drizzle over the olive oil and season with salt and pepper. Toss lightly in the oil and then fold over the foil to make a loose parcel. Bake in the oven for 45–50 minutes until the beetroot is cooked. When cool enough to handle, peel and cut the beetroot into wedges.

Whisk all the dressing ingredients together (or shake in a screw-topped jar), adding the cooked crushed garlic to the dressing.

Place the rocket or watercress on plates and top with the tofu pieces and roasted vegetables. Scatter over the hazelnuts and drizzle over the dressing to serve.

Per serving: 412 kcal; 17.4g protein; 30.2g fat; 2.9g saturated fat; 14.1g carbohydrates; 10.9g sugars

Miso Quinoa Bowl

This power-packed miso bowl is such a quick and easy dish to make for lunch or dinner. You can pre-cook the quinoa and keep it in the fridge ready for speedy dishes like this one. Miso is a delicious fermented soy product that gives a wonderful salty umami flavour to dishes. Serve this warm or cold.

PREPARATION TIME: 15 minutes
COOKING TIME: 30 minutes
SERVES 4

1 head of broccoli (250g), cut into florets
2 tbsp olive oil
150g quinoa, ideally soaked in cold water for 30 minutes
700ml vegetable stock
100g frozen edamame (soybeans)
150g shiitake mushrooms, sliced
3 spring onions, chopped
2 large handfuls (50g) of rocket or watercress
1 tbsp chopped fresh coriander leaves
1 tbsp sesame seeds
1 tbsp pumpkin seeds

For the lemon miso dressing
2 tbsp white miso paste

1 garlic clove, crushed
1 tsp grated fresh ginger
2 tbsp mirin
1 tbsp tamari soy sauce
2 tbsp rice wine vinegar
2 tsp xylitol or granulated stevia, or to taste
Zest and juice of 1 lemon
1 tbsp water

Preheat the oven to 180°C/fan 160°C/gas mark 4. Place the broccoli on a baking tray and drizzle over 1 tbsp of the olive oil. Roast in the oven for 30 minutes until the broccoli is just slightly golden.

Meanwhile rinse the quinoa well and place in a pan with the vegetable stock. Bring to the boil, then reduce the heat and simmer over a very low heat for 15 minutes until cooked. Turn off the heat but leave the lid on to let the quinoa steam for a further 5 minutes.

Pour boiling water over the edamame beans and leave for 5 minutes, then drain. Whisk together the ingredients for the miso dressing (or shake in a screw-topped jar).

Heat the remaining oil in the frying pan and sauté the mushrooms, spring onions and edamame beans over a medium heat for 2 minutes until softened. Pour over the miso dressing and heat through for a minute.

Divide the cooked quinoa between four bowls and top with the rocket or watercress leaves, roasted broccoli and mushroom mixture. Scatter with the coriander and serve.

Per serving: 286 kcal; 15.6g protein; 12.9g fat; 1.8g saturated fat; 27.1g carbohydrates; 4.5g sugars

Tamari-Marinated Mushrooms and Mixed Bean Salad

This super speedy dish requires just a little preparation the day before to really boost the flavours – the mushrooms soften in the tangy soy marinade and readily absorb the flavours. Making use of tinned cooked beans makes this quick and easy to prepare.

PREPARATION TIME: 10 minutes, plus marinating
COOKING TIME: 7 minutes
SERVES 4

400g chestnut mushrooms, sliced
1 red onion, diced
4 tbsp balsamic vinegar
4 tbsp tamari soy sauce
2 tsp xylitol
1 garlic clove, crushed
1 tbsp coconut oil
300g green beans
3 x 400g tins mixed beans, rinsed and drained
200g mixed leafy salad greens

Place the mushrooms and onion in a shallow bowl and pour over the vinegar, soy sauce and xylitol. Stir in the garlic and leave to marinate for at least 1 hour, ideally overnight.

Meanwhile bring a pan of water to the boil. Add the green beans, cover and cook for 4–5 minutes until tender. Drain and refresh under cold water, then drain again.

Melt the coconut oil in a pan over a medium heat and add the mushrooms and onion along with the marinade. Cover the pan and simmer over a low heat for 2 minutes to soften the mushrooms.

Place the green beans and tinned mixed beans in a large bowl with the salad greens. Top with the mushroom and onion mixture and toss gently to combine. Serve warm or cold.

Per serving: 278 kcal; 17.7g protein; 4.1g fat; 2.3g saturated fat; 33.6g carbohydrates; 6.1g sugars

Pomegranate-glazed Aubergine Lentil Salad

Thick sweet slices of aubergine are griddled until golden and served with a tangy pomegranate dressing. These are delicious warm topped with a little herby yoghurt. Baharat is a spice mixture usually including coriander, cumin, cinnamon, cayenne pepper, cloves, nutmeg and cardamom. If you cannot find it use a little cumin and coriander instead. Using ready-cooked lentils is a quick way to add more protein to the salad but you can use 190g dried lentils and cook them yourself, following the packet instructions.

PREPARATION TIME: 10 minutes, plus marinating
COOKING TIME: 6 minutes
SERVES 4

2 medium aubergines
Olive oil, for frying
600g cooked puy lentils
100g mixed salad leaves
4 spring onions, chopped
1 red chilli, deseeded and diced
30g pomegranate seeds
Handful of chopped fresh coriander leaves

For the marinade
3 tbsp tamari soy sauce
1 tsp baharat spice mix
Juice of 2 pomegranates (about 120ml)
1 tsp ground cinnamon
2 garlic cloves, crushed
1 tbsp lemon juice
½ tsp ground cumin
1 tsp xylitol
1 tsp olive oil
Sea salt and black pepper

Slice the aubergine into rounds about 1cm thick and place in a shallow dish. Mix together all the marinade ingredients and pour over the aubergines. Place in the fridge to marinate for at least 2–3 hours, preferably overnight.

Heat a griddle pan or frying pan over a medium-high heat and drizzle lightly with olive oil. Remove the aubergine from the marinade and reserve the marinade. Add the aubergine slices to the hot pan and cook in batches for 2–3 minutes each side until golden.

Add the reserved marinade to the cooked and drained lentils. Warm through over a low heat for a minute or two.

Arrange the salad greens on four plates and top with the lentils, aubergine slices, spring onions, red chilli, pomegranate seeds and chopped coriander.

Per serving: 251 kcal; 15.7g protein; 3.3g fat; 0.5g saturated fat; 33.9g carbohydrates; 8.8g sugars

Waldorf Salad with Smoked Tofu

The creamy dressing has an avocado base, which provides protein and healthy monounsaturated fats. It is equally good drizzled over cooked vegetables too. Smoked tofu is readily available in supermarkets and has a wonderful earthy flavour.

PREPARATION TIME: 15 minutes
COOKING TIME: 5 minutes
SERVES 4

1 tbsp olive oil or coconut oil
600g smoked tofu, cut into 1cm cubes
2 heads of romaine lettuce, shredded
Large handful of watercress
Large handful of rocket leaves or baby spinach
4 celery sticks, sliced
1 small green apple, cored and diced
100g seedless red grapes, halved
1 tbsp chopped fresh parsley
30g macadamia nuts
2 tbsp nutritional yeast flakes

For the dressing
1 ripe avocado, roughly chopped
½–1 tsp Dijon mustard
2 tbsp apple cider vinegar

3–4 tbsp water
½ tsp garlic or onion salt
1 tbsp nutritional yeast flakes
Sea salt and black pepper

Heat a frying pan and add the oil. Fry the smoked tofu pieces over a medium heat until golden and crisp, about 5 minutes. Remove from the pan and set aside.

Place the shredded lettuce, watercress and spinach in a bowl and add the celery, apple and grapes. Scatter over the parsley and tofu pieces.

Put all the dressing ingredients into a blender and blend until smooth, adding just enough of the water to make a thick dressing. Season to taste and then pour over the salad and toss lightly to combine.

Use a microplane to grate the macadamia nuts into a bowl. Mix in the yeast flakes and then sprinkle over the salad to serve.

Per serving: 309 kcal; 18.3g protein; 19.9g fat; 3g saturated fat; 11.1g carbohydrates; 8g sugars

Noodle Pot Salad

This is a fabulous packed lunch dish to go – when you are ready to eat simply pour over a little boiling water to make a soupy salad. Just pack everything into a large jar or Tupperware container and keep in the fridge until ready to eat. Using vegetables to create noodles keeps the carbohydrate levels down, but you can also use soaked and drained kelp noodles, which also provide plenty of thyroid-supporting iodine.

PREPARATION TIME: 10 minutes
SERVES 2

1 medium courgette or 60g kelp noodles
1 carrot
2 spring onions, chopped
Small handful of mixed sea vegetables or 1 sheet of nori, crumbled
1 tsp grated fresh ginger
1 tbsp white miso paste
1 pak choi, finely shredded
4 mushrooms, sliced
100g cooked edamame (soybeans)
8 sugar snap peas or mangetout, sliced
1 tbsp tamari soy sauce
1 tbsp lime or lemon juice

Use a spiraliser or swivel potato peeler to make long noodles from the courgette and carrot. If using the kelp noodles soak according to the packet instructions then drain.

Place the noodles in your chosen container along with all the remaining ingredients and place in the fridge until needed.

When you are ready to eat, simply pour over a little boiling water, just to cover everything. Leave to sit for 6–8 minutes, pressing the mixture down under the water. Stir gently before eating.

Per serving: 168 kcal; 14.5g protein; 5.8g fat; 0.7g saturated fat; 14g carbohydrates; 10.3g sugars

Easy Asian Chopped Salad

This is a great filling salad, which can be varied according to the season – when in season try adding some steamed asparagus or purple sprouting broccoli. Assemble the salad ahead of time and keep in the fridge, then dress just before serving.

PREPARATION TIME: 15 minutes
SERVES 4

3 tomatoes, deseeded and diced
1 red pepper, diced
1 cucumber, halved lengthways, deseeded and diced
1 little gem lettuce, shredded
2 spring onions, thinly sliced
100g red cabbage, grated or shredded
½ ripe avocado, diced
2 x 400g tins butterbeans, rinsed and drained
1 tbsp chopped fresh parsley
1 tbsp chopped fresh mint leaves
30g toasted and salted cashew nuts

For the dressing
½ shallot, finely chopped
3 tbsp tamari soy sauce
2 tbsp rice wine vinegar
Juice of ½ orange

1 tsp xylitol or granulated stevia
1 tsp grated fresh ginger
Pinch of dried chilli flakes
Pinch of Chinese five-spice powder
Sea salt and black pepper

Blend or whisk all the dressing ingredients together (or shake in a screw-topped jar).

Place all the salad ingredients except the herbs and cashews into a large bowl, and drizzle over the dressing. Toss lightly to coat. Top with the herbs and cashew nuts and serve.

Per serving: 211 kcal; 11.1g protein; 7.3g fat; 1.5g saturated fat; 24.9g carbohydrates; 9g sugars

Spicy Walnut Lettuce Cups with Lime Yoghurt Dressing

Using little gem leaves as wraps is a great low-carb option. This salad is full of Mexican flavours and makes an ideal lunch or dinner option. Walnuts are a good source of Omega-3 fats but you could make the chunky filling with other nuts or sunflower seeds too.

PREPARATION TIME: 15 minutes, plus soaking
SERVES 4

100g walnuts, ideally soaked in water for 2 hours and drained
60g sun-dried tomatoes, drained
1 tsp ground cumin
1/2 tsp garlic salt
½ tsp ground coriander
½ tsp chilli powder
½ tsp smoked paprika
30g soft dates, chopped
1 tbsp tamari soy sauce
2–3 tablespoons water
2 x 400g tin kidney beans, rinsed and drained
2 tomatoes, deseeded and chopped
2 little gem lettuces, to serve

For the lime yoghurt dressing
1 garlic clove, chopped

150g coconut yoghurt, shop-bought or homemade (see page 81)
Juice of 1 lime
½ tsp xylitol
1 tbsp chopped fresh coriander leaves
Sea salt and black pepper

To make the filling place all filling ingredients except the beans and tomatoes into a food processor and process briefly to form a crumbly texture, adding just enough water to combine. Add the beans and tomato and pulse again to form a chunky mixture.

To make the dressing, place all the ingredients in a blender and whizz until smooth.

Separate out the lettuce leaves. Place spoonfuls of the taco mixture into each lettuce leaf and top with a spoonful of lime dressing.

Per serving: 485 kcal; 15g protein; 32.8g fat; 9g saturated fat; 26.4g carbohydrates; 9g sugars

Roasted Cauliflower and Pistachio Tabbouleh

Using cauliflower to replace grains makes this a wonderful low-carb and filling dish. For additional protein serve this salad with around 150g cooked beans, lentils or tofu

PREPARATION TIME: 10 minutes
COOKING TIME: 30 minutes
SERVES 4

1 head of cauliflower, outer leaves removed
Olive oil, for drizzling
60g pistachio nuts
1 onion, diced
1 tsp ground cumin
1 cucumber, deseeded and diced
4 tomatoes, deseeded and diced
2 tsp coconut oil, melted
30g pomegranate seeds
Sea salt and black pepper

For the dressing
Juice of 2 lemons
100ml olive oil or flaxseed oil
1 tsp xylitol
Handful of mint leaves, chopped

Handful of fresh parsley chopped
Sea salt and black pepper

Preheat the oven to 200°C/fan 180°C fan/gas mark 6.

Cut the cauliflower into two and place one half in a food processor and blitz to form fine 'rice'-like grains. Tip in a large bowl.

Cut the remaining cauliflower into very small florets. Place the florets on a baking tray, drizzle with a little olive oil and season with salt and pepper. Roast in the oven for 20–30 minutes until golden and slightly crisp. Set aside to cool.

Meanwhile place the pistachio nuts in a dry frying pan and toast over a gentle heat for 2–3 minutes. Place in the food processor and pulse lightly to chop coarsely. Add to the cauliflower rice, along with the cooled roasted cauliflower and all the remaining ingredients. Stir gently to combine.

To make the dressing, place all the ingredients in a food processor or blender and whizz to combine. Pour over the salad and toss to coat.

Per serving: 404 kcal; 8.7g protein; 36.3g fat; 6.3g saturated fat; 11g carbohydrates; 8.8g sugars

Nori Avocado Rolls

This is a vegan version of sushi. Using parsnip or cauliflower makes a delicious alternative to regular rice and keeps the dish lower in carbohydrates and higher in protein. Make up a big batch of the rice and keep in the fridge to use as an accompaniment to other dishes.

PREPARATION TIME: 20 minutes
SERVES 2

4 nori sheets
½ red pepper, thinly sliced
1 carrot, thinly sliced
Handful of mung beansprouts or other sprouts
½ avocado, thinly sliced

For the rice
200g parsnips, peeled and chopped or ½ small cauliflower, broken into florets
1 tbsp white miso paste
30g sunflower seeds
1 tsp rice wine vinegar
1 tbsp tamari soy sauce

For the peanut dipping sauce
4 tbsp tamari soy sauce

2 tbsp lime juice
1 tbsp smooth peanut butter
2 tsp xylitol or granulated stevia, or to taste
½ garlic clove, crushed
1 tsp grated fresh ginger

Make up the dipping sauce by mixing together all the ingredients to form a thick sauce.

To make the rice blitz the parsnip or cauliflower in a food processor until you have a rice-like consistency. Add the remaining ingredients and process briefly together.

Assemble the rolls: lay out one sheet of the nori, place a couple of large spoonfuls of the 'rice' along the bottom half side of the nori sheet and press down lightly. Layer a few strips of red pepper, carrot, sprouts and avocado over the rice. Dab the sides and edges of the nori sheet with a little water then tightly roll up the nori to form a tight roll.

Dip a serrated knife in water then slice the nori roll into large pieces to serve. Repeat with the remaining nori sheets and fillings. Serve with the peanut dipping sauce.

Per serving: 328 kcal; 12.6g protein; 18g fat; 3g saturated fat; 29.8g carbohydrates; 14.3g sugars

Coconut Dahl with Wilted Greens

A simple, warming dish that is made light and creamy by the addition of coconut milk. To save time you can replace the spices with a prepared curry paste. For a more substantial meal, serve with cooked quinoa or brown rice.

PREPARATION TIME: 10 minutes
COOKING TIME: 35–40 minutes
SERVES 4

250g split red lentils
1 cinnamon stick
200ml coconut milk
1 tsp cumin seeds
1 tbsp coconut oil
1 onion, diced
2 garlic cloves, crushed
1 tsp grated fresh ginger
1 tsp ground turmeric
1 tsp garam masala
1 tsp ground coriander
1 tsp mustard seeds
2 dried curry leaves
2 tomatoes, chopped
200g baby spinach
Chopped coriander, to serve

Rinse the lentils in water and then place in a large pan with the cinnamon stick. Cover with water and bring to the boil, then reduce the heat and simmer for about 30 minutes until tender. Drain the lentils and return to the pan with the coconut milk. Simmer, covered, for 2–3 minutes.

Meanwhile fry the cumin seeds in a dry frying pan over a medium heat for a couple of minutes to toast lightly. Add the coconut oil, onion, garlic and ginger and sauté for 5 minutes until the onion is soft and lightly golden.

Add the remaining spices, curry leaves, tomatoes and spinach and cook for a further 5 minutes. Tip this spice mixture into the pan of lentils and stir to combine. Heat through then divide between bowls and serve with a little chopped coriander

Per serving: 262 kcal; 17.5g protein; 4.2g fat; 2.3g saturated fat; 39.6g carbohydrates; 7.5g sugars

RECIPES
Veggie Mains

Cauliflower and Tofu Fried Rice

Cauliflower is so versatile and is ideal for replacing grains in recipes. Simply blitzing it in a food processor to create 'rice' allows you to use it in a wide range of dishes when you want to keep the carbohydrate content down. This is equally delicious eaten cold the following day.

PREPARATION TIME: 10 minutes
COOKING TIME: 10–12 minutes
SERVES 4

1 medium head of cauliflower, broken into florets
2 tbsp sesame seeds
1 tbsp coconut oil
600g firm tofu, drained and cut into 2cm cubes
½ red onion, finely chopped
1 garlic clove, crushed
1 tsp grated fresh ginger
100g shiitake mushrooms, sliced
1 medium courgette, diced
½ red pepper, diced
2 tbsp tamari soy sauce
1 tsp rice wine vinegar
1 tbsp mirin
2 spring onions, thinly sliced
Handful of chopped fresh coriander leaves

Handful of chopped fresh basil leaves
Handful of chopped fresh mint leaves
Sea salt and black pepper

Put the cauliflower in a food processor and pulse until you have fine 'grains'. Set aside. Place a frying pan over a medium heat and add the sesame seeds. Toast for a minute until golden then remove from the pan.

Heat the coconut oil in the same pan and sauté the tofu for 5 minutes each side until lightly golden. Add the onion, garlic and ginger and cook for 1 minute.

Add the mushrooms, courgette, red pepper and cauliflower rice, season with salt and pepper and then pour over the tamari, vinegar, mirin, spring onions and herbs. Place a lid on the pan and steam-fry for 5 minutes. Scatter over the toasted sesame seeds and serve immediately.

Per serving: 236 kcal; 18.1g protein; 13.6g fat; 3.6g saturated fat; 8.3g carbohydrates; 5.9g sugars

Tex Mex Burgers with Spicy Chilli Dressing

These vegan burgers are wonderfully fragrant with Mexican spices. The beans provide plenty of protein while the oats are rich in soluble fibre to help stabilise blood sugar levels and support digestive health. Using flaxseed is another great way to bind dishes together without the need for eggs. Top with a spoonful of the tangy dressing.

PREPARATION TIME: 20 minutes
COOKING TIME: 10 minutes
MAKES 4

For the burgers
2 garlic cloves, chopped
½ small onion, chopped
1 tsp xylitol
2 tsp smoked paprika
1 tsp ground cumin
½ tsp chilli powder
1 tsp dried oregano
2 tbsp tomato purée
1 tbsp tamari soy sauce
2 tbsp ground flaxseed or chia seeds
1 x 400g tin butterbeans
75g gluten-free oats

50g tinned or frozen and thawed sweetcorn
Sea salt and black pepper

For the spicy chilli dressing
125g sunflower seeds
1 tsp smoked paprika
1 tbsp lemon juice
1 pickled chilli, drained and chopped
¼ tsp salt
1 roasted red pepper (from a jar), drained
3–4 tbsp water

Place all the burger ingredients except the butterbeans, oats and sweetcorn in a food processor and blitz to form a thick paste. Add the beans, oats and sweetcorn and pulse briefly, just to combine everything but still keeping some texture. Season with salt and pepper. Divide the mixture into four, then wet your hands and shape into burgers.

Preheat the grill to high. Place the burgers on a non-stick baking tray and grill for 5 minutes on each side until golden and crisp.

To make the spicy dressing simply place all the ingredients in a blender and blitz, adding just enough water to create a thick sauce.

Serve the burgers topped with a spoonful of the dressing and accompany with mixed salad or steamed vegetables.

Per serving: 384 kcal; 15.3g protein; 20.8g fat; 2.5g saturated fat; 35g carbohydrates; 5.3g sugars

Courgette Carbonara

A simple, low-carb comfort dish that is easy to prepare and delicious accompanied with a simple mixed salad. You can make the 'cheese' sauce in advance and keep in the fridge for 2–3 days if wished.

PREPARATION TIME: 15 minutes, plus soaking
COOKING TIME: 8 minutes
SERVES 2

2 medium courgettes
1 carrot
100g frozen edamame (soybeans) or cooked drained cannellini beans
1 tsp coconut oil
½ red onion, diced
1 garlic clove, crushed
100g button mushrooms, chopped
100g baby spinach leaves
Black pepper
2 tbsp chopped fresh parsley

For the sauce
80g cashew nuts, ideally soaked in cold water for 2 hours
80g macadamia nuts, ideally soaked in cold water for 2 hours
Juice of ½ lemon

1 tbsp tamari soy sauce
3 tbsp nutritional yeast flakes
Sea salt and black pepper

First make the sauce. Rinse and drain the nuts then place in a high-speed blender with all the other ingredients and process until smooth, adding enough water to make a thick, pourable sauce.

Spiralise the courgettes and carrot to form long noodles. Alternatively use a swivel potato peeler and create long ribbons instead.

If using edamame beans, blanch them in a bowl of boiling water for 5 minutes or until just soft, then drain.

Melt the coconut oil in a large pan over a medium heat and add the onion, garlic and mushrooms. Sauté for a couple of minutes to soften. Add the drained edamame or cannellini beans and spinach and stir until the spinach has wilted. Stir in the sauce and the noodles and toss everything together to coat.

Spoon into two bowls and top each with a little black pepper and some chopped parsley.

Per serving: 419 kcal; 19.5g protein; 31.9g fat; 6.2g saturated fat; 13.3g carbohydrates; 7.1g sugars

Pea Falafels with Tzatziki

Peas are a good source of protein for vegans and using frozen peas makes this an easy dish to prepare. Serve with the Roasted Root Hummus (see page 244) and a mixed salad for a more substantial dish. These falafels could also be served cold with a few salad leaves for an easy portable lunch option.

PREPARATION TIME: 15 minutes
COOKING TIME: 30 minutes
MAKES 12 falafels (to serve 3)

150g frozen peas, cooked and drained
1 x 400g tin chickpeas, rinsed and drained
2 tbsp gram (chickpea) flour
1 tbsp chopped fresh parsley
1 tbsp chopped fresh mint
1 garlic clove, crushed
1 tsp ground cumin
1 tbsp tahini paste
2 tbsp lemon juice
Sea salt and black pepper
Olive oil, for brushing

For the tzatziki
150g coconut yoghurt, shop-bought or homemade (see page 81)

2 tbsp chopped fresh mint
1 tbsp lemon juice
100g cucumber (about 1/3), grated
Sea salt and black pepper

Preheat the oven to 200°C/fan 180°C/gas mark 6 and line a baking tray with baking parchment.

Place all the ingredients except the olive oil in a food processor and pulse until everything is combined but still has some texture. You may need to scrape down the side of the bowl with a spatula a couple of times.

Using slightly wet hands, roll the mixture into 12 small balls. Place the balls on the lined baking tray. Brush or drizzle the falafels with a little olive oil and then bake in the oven for 15 minutes before turning them over and returning to the oven for a further 10–15 minutes, or until golden.

Meanwhile make the tzatziki: place the yoghurt, mint, lemon juice and salt and pepper in a blender and blitz to combine. Stir in the cucumber and then serve with the warm falafels.

Per serving: 206 kcal; 12.4g protein; 6.7g fat; 0.9g saturated fat; 24.4g carbohydrates; 4.8g sugars

Vegan Bolognese with Vegetable Noodles

If you miss spaghetti and meat sauce then try this healthy, low-carb alternative. If you can't get hold of tempeh use tofu or substitute a couple of cans of cooked beans to increase the protein content.

PREPARATION TIME: 15 minutes
COOKING TIME: 30 minutes
SERVES 4

1 tbsp coconut oil
1 small onion, finely chopped
1 garlic clove, crushed
1/2 red pepper, finely chopped
1 small carrot, finely chopped
1 celery stick, finely chopped
½ tsp smoked paprika
1 tsp ground cumin
150g button mushrooms, sliced
400g tempeh or tofu, crumbled or 2 x 400g tins kidney
    beans, rinsed and drained
1 tsp dried oregano
30g split red lentils
50g tomato purée
1 x 400g tin chopped tomatoes

100ml vegetable stock
Handful of fresh parsley, chopped
4 small courgettes
Sea salt and black pepper

Heat the oil in a large pan over a medium heat. Add the onion, garlic, pepper, carrot, celery and spices and sauté for 5 minutes, stirring occasionally.

Add the mushrooms and tempeh or tofu (or kidney beans) and cook for another 5 minutes.

Add the oregano, lentils, tomato purée, chopped tomatoes and vegetable stock. Bring to a simmer and then cook, covered, for 20 minutes until the lentils are soft. Add the fresh parsley and season to taste.

Use a spiraliser to make long noodles from the courgettes. If wished steam the courgette noodles for a couple of minutes to soften. Spoon the noodles into bowls and top with the sauce.

Per serving: 296 kcal; 28.4g protein; 10.3g fat; 2.2g saturated fat; 22.2g carbohydrates; 12.1g sugars

Fennel, Tomato and Bean Crumble Bake

This Italian-style dish is light and refreshing and delicious served hot or cold. The beans provide plenty of fibre and protein, making this a filling and satisfying dish.

PREPARATION TIME: 10 minutes
COOKING TIME: 40–45 minutes
SERVES 4

1 tbsp coconut or olive oil
1 onion, finely chopped
3 garlic cloves, crushed
3 small fennel bulbs, trimmed and thinly sliced
1 tsp fresh thyme leaves
1 x 400g tin chopped tomatoes
150g cherry tomatoes, halved
1 x 400g tin butterbeans or cannellini beans, rinsed and
  drained
100g gluten-free oats
30g sunflower seeds
2 tbsp nutritional yeast flakes
Sea salt and black pepper

Preheat the oven to 200°C/fan 180°C/gas mark 6.

Heat the oil in a large pan and gently sauté the onion and garlic over a medium heat for 2–3 minutes. Add the sliced fennel and thyme leaves and cook for a further 5 minutes, turning them occasionally in the pan. Season with salt and pepper.

Add the chopped tomatoes, cherry tomatoes and beans to the pan. Cover and simmer for about 5 minutes until the fennel has softened. Transfer the vegetables to an ovenproof dish.

Mix the oats, sunflower seeds and nutritional yeast flakes together and sprinkle over the top of the vegetables. Bake in the oven for 20–30 minutes until the oat topping is lightly golden.

Per serving: 269 kcal; 13g protein; 8.9g fat; 2.5g saturated fat; 33.7g carbohydrates; 8.3g sugars

Vegan Meatballs with Barbecue Tomato Sauce

These meatballs are a comforting family favourite and the barbecue sauce is also delicious poured over courgette noodles, cooked quinoa or as an accompaniment to burgers (see page 187). Make up a big batch of the sauce and keep in the freezer for up to 3 months.

PREPARATION TIME: 15 minutes
COOKING TIME: 30 minutes
SERVES 4

100g gluten-free oats
1 tbsp flaxseed soaked in 2 tbsp water
½ red onion, finely chopped
2 garlic cloves, finely chopped
2 sun-dried tomatoes
1 tbsp chopped fresh basil
1 x 400g tin kidney beans, rinsed and drained
Sea salt and black pepper
1 tbsp coconut oil
3 medium courgettes

For the barbecue sauce
1 tbsp coconut oil
½ red onion, chopped

1 garlic clove, crushed

½ tsp Dijon mustard

1 tsp xylitol

125g sun-dried tomatoes in oil, drained

1 x 400g tin chopped tomatoes

4 dates

2 tbsp apple cider vinegar

2 tbsp tamari soy sauce

½ tsp smoked paprika

Pinch of chilli flakes

Sea salt and black pepper

First make the sauce. Place all the ingredients in a food processor or blender and blitz until smooth. Pour into a pan and simmer gently for 5 minutes. Set aside.

To make the meatballs place all the ingredients except the coconut oil and courgettes in a food processor and pulse until the mixture comes together – you want to keep a little texture. Take small pieces of the mixture and roll into walnut-sized balls. You should get around 16 small balls.

Preheat the oven to 180°C/fan 160°C/gas mark 4 and line a baking tray with baking parchment. Place a frying pan over a medium heat and add half the coconut oil. When the pan is hot add half of the meatballs and cook for about 5 minutes, give the pan a shake occasionally to roll the meatballs so that they brown all over (turn down the heat if they appear to be browning too quickly). Transfer to the baking tray and repeat with the remaining meatballs. Place the baking tray in the oven and bake for 10–15 minutes until golden and crisp.

Gently heat the sauce and add the meatballs. Toss to coat in the sauce.

Spiralise the courgettes, or use a vegetable peeler to cut them into long ribbons, and steam for 2 minutes. Meanwhile gently reheat the barbecue sauce and add the cooked meatballs. Toss to coat the meatballs in the sauce. Divide the courgettes between four plates and top each with a generous helping of meatballs and sauce.

Per serving: 255 kcal; 11.5g protein; 6.8g fat; 1.2g saturated fat; 36.7g carbohydrates; 11.2g sugars

Pesto-stuffed Portobello Mushrooms

Portobello mushrooms are rich and juicy and make the ideal base for filling with this delicious vegan pesto. These are delicious served hot or cold, with some cooked beans or tofu for additional protein.

PREPARATION TIME: 15 minutes
COOKING TIME: 13 minutes
SERVES 4

1 tbsp olive oil
8 Portobello mushrooms, stalks removed
8 tbsp tomato sauce or passata
30g black olives, chopped
½ red pepper, diced
1 tomato, deseeded and diced

For the vegan pesto
100g cashew nuts
1 garlic clove, crushed
2 tbsp nutritional yeast flakes
Large handful (30g) of basil leaves
2 tbsp lemon juice
4–5 tbsp water
Sea salt and black pepper

First make the pesto. Place all the ingredients in a high-speed blender and process until smooth, adding just enough water to create a thick paste. Season to taste with salt and pepper.

Preheat the grill to high and line a baking tray with baking parchment.

Heat the olive oil in a pan and add the whole mushrooms. Cover the pan and cook for 2–3 minutes just to soften the mushrooms slightly. Remove from the pan then place the mushrooms cap side up on the lined baking sheet.

Spoon the tomato sauce or passata over each of the mushrooms and top with a spoonful of the pesto. Scatter the olives, pepper and tomato over the tops.

Place the mushrooms under the grill and cook for about 10 minutes until the sauce is bubbling and the mushroom tops have turned lightly golden.

Per serving: 207 kcal; 9.5g protein; 13.6g fat; 2.6g saturated fat; 11.5g carbohydrates; 6.6g sugars

Chickpea Pancakes with Spiced Tomato and Bean Chutney

Gram, or chickpea flour is a great protein option and is traditionally used to make Indian breads and pancakes or fritters. You can prepare the batter the day before and store in the fridge until required. The chutney will also keep in the fridge for a week, making this the perfect standby dinner option. Simply serve with steamed greens and a mixed salad.

PREPARATION TIME: 15 minutes
COOKING TIME: 25 minutes
SERVES 2

70g gram (chickpea) flour
100ml water
½ red onion, grated
½ tsp ground cumin
¼ tsp ground turmeric
¼ tsp onion powder
Pinch of chilli flakes
½ tsp baking powder
¼ tsp sea salt
Handful of fresh coriander leaves, chopped
1 tsp olive oil, plus extra for frying
½ ripe avocado, to serve
Mixed salad leaves, to serve

For the chutney
1 tsp coconut oil
1/2 teaspoon mustard seeds
1 tsp cumin seeds
½ onion, finely chopped
1 garlic clove, crushed
1 tsp grated fresh ginger
1 green chilli, deseeded and chopped
3 tomatoes, deseeded and chopped
1 x 400g tin kidney beans, rinsed and drained
1/4 tsp ground turmeric
½ tsp ground coriander
1 tbsp apple cider vinegar
1 tsp xylitol
Pinch of sea salt

First make the chutney. Heat the oil in a pan and add the mustard and cumin seeds. Put the lid on the pan and let them crackle for a minute. Add all the remaining ingredients and cook over a low heat, covered, for about 10 minutes until the tomatoes and soft and mushy. Set aside.

In a bowl, combine the chickpea flour and water (you may not need all of it), whisking to create a smooth batter, about the consistency of double cream. Stir in all the remaining ingredients and allow the batter to sit for 5 minutes.

Place a frying pan over a medium heat. When hot, drizzle a few drops of oil in the pan, swirling it over the base of the pan. Pour a spoonful of the batter into the frying pan and again, swirl the batter around the pan to make a small pancake. Cook until the edges of the pancake begin to turn lightly golden, about 2–3 minutes. Flip the pancake over and cook for a further 2–3 minutes. Remove from the pan and repeat with the remaining batter to make four small pancakes.

Serve the pancakes with salad, sliced avocado and the chutney.

Per serving: 356 kcal; 18.1g protein; 11.6g fat; 3g saturated fat; 46.2g carbohydrates; 11.2g sugars

Buckwheat, Mushroom and Spinach Risotto

This creamy and comforting risotto makes a perfect warming dinner and is delicious topped with some cooked lentils or beans for additional protein. Using buckwheat instead of rice means you will increase your intake of protein, as well as valuable vitamins and minerals, including magnesium for energy production and bone health.

PREPARATION TIME: 15 minutes, plus soaking
COOKING TIME: 30 minutes
SERVES 4

15g dried mushrooms
1 tbsp coconut oil
1 red onion, diced
3 celery sticks, diced
2 garlic cloves, crushed
450g mixed mushrooms, sliced and stalks chopped
125g asparagus, diagonally sliced into 2cm pieces
160g buckwheat, soaked in water for 30 minutes and drained
400ml vegetable stock
100g baby spinach leaves
Juice of ½ lemon
Sea salt and black pepper
2 tbsp nutritional yeast flakes (optional)

Put the dried mushrooms in a bowl and cover with about 150ml boiling water. Leave to soak for 15 minutes.

Heat the oil in a large pan over a medium heat and gently fry the onion, celery and garlic for 10 minutes until soft. Add the mixed mushrooms and asparagus and stir to coat in the oil. Add the buckwheat and stir for a minute before pouring in the stock. Bring to the boil, then reduce the heat, cover and simmer 15 minutes – the buckwheat should be just tender.

Drain the dried mushrooms (reserving the liquid) and chop. Add to the pan, along with the soaking liquid, and cook for a further 5 minutes with the pan uncovered until the buckwheat is cooked through and very soft. Stir through the spinach and allow it to wilt in the heat.

Add the lemon juice, seasoning and nutritional yeast flakes, if using. Serve immediately.

Per serving: 234 kcal; 10.4g protein; 4.5g fat; 2.2g saturated fat; 37.8g carbohydrates; 3.8g sugars

Sweet Potato and Lentil Moussaka

A delicious warming dish that is perfect for making in advance. It also freezes well, making it a great option for a standby dinner. Packed with flavour this is an ideal family dish and great for entertaining.

PREPARATION TIME: 15 minutes
COOKING TIME: 1 hour
SERVES 4

1 medium aubergine
1 medium courgette
Olive oil, for brushing
300g sweet potato, peeled and thinly sliced
Sea salt

For the tomato and lentil sauce
1 tbsp olive oil
1 onion, diced
2 garlic cloves, crushed
2 tbsp tomato purée
75g red split lentils
250ml vegetable stock
1 x 400g tin chopped tomatoes
1 tsp dried oregano

1/4 tsp ground cinnamon
Sea salt and black pepper

For the cashew cream topping
60g cashew nuts
1 tbsp gram (chickpea) flour
Juice of 1 lemon
1 tsp xylitol
350g soft silken tofu
½ tsp garlic salt
¼ tsp cayenne pepper
2 tbsp nutritional yeast flakes

First make the tomato sauce. Heat the oil in a pan over a medium heat and add the onion and garlic. Sauté for 5 minutes then add the remaining ingredients. Bring to a simmer and cook for 15 minutes until the lentils are cooked. Season to taste.

Meanwhile preheat oven to 190°C/fan 170°C/gas mark 5. Slice the aubergine and courgette to form rounds about 1cm thick. Lay the slices on a grill rack inside a baking tin and brush the tops with a little olive oil. Sprinkle lightly with sea salt and roast in the oven until soft and lightly browned, about 15 minutes.

Bring a pan of salted water to the boil and add the sweet potato slices. Parboil for about 5 minutes, then drain and set aside.

Place the cashew nuts in a food processor or blender and process until fine. Add all the remaining topping ingredients and blend to form a thick sauce.

To assemble the moussaka, layer a little of the tomato sauce in the base of a baking dish, then place a layer of aubergine and courgette followed by a layer of sweet potato. Repeat these layers until the ingredients are all used up, then finish with the cashew cream topping. Bake in the oven for 30–40 minutes until the top is golden.

Per serving: 381 kcal; 20.9g protein; 15.6g fat; 2.5g saturated fat; 39.6g carbohydrates; 12.3g sugars

Black Bean, Shiitake and Red Pepper Stir-Fry

This recipe is so easy to assemble and packed with flavour. Using tahini is a wonderful way to create a vegan creamy sauce and is a great source of calcium. If you are short of time you can use a bag of ready-prepared stir-fry vegetables instead. Serve this with spiralised courgettes or kelp noodles to boost your iodine intake.

PREPARATION TIME: 15 minutes
COOKING TIME: 6 minutes
SERVES 4

1 tbsp coconut oil
4 spring onions, sliced
1 garlic clove, crushed
1 red pepper, thinly sliced
1 carrot, julienned
Handful of sea vegetables (soaked and drained) or 1 sheet of nori, crumbled
300g shiitake mushrooms, sliced
Handful of mangetout
2 x 400g tins black beans, rinsed and drained or 400g cooked edamame (soybeans)
Handful of beansprouts
1 tbsp sesame seeds
Handful of coriander leaves, chopped

2 large courgettes, spiralised or 150g soaked and drained kelp noodles, to serve

For the sauce
2 tbsp light miso
2 tbsp rice wine vinegar
1 tbsp tahini paste
1 tbsp tamari soy sauce
Juice of 1 orange

First make up the sauce – simply whisk all the ingredients together in a bowl until smooth.

Heat the coconut oil in a wok or frying pan. Add the spring onions and garlic and stir-fry for 1 minute. Add the pepper, carrot, sea vegetables, mushrooms and mangetout and fry for 2–3 minutes to soften slightly. Add the beans and beansprouts and pour over the sauce. Toss the vegetables to coat in the sauce and heat through for 1–2 minutes.

Scatter over the sesame seeds and coriander to serve.

Per serving (without noodles): 244 kcal; 13.5g protein; 8.4g fat; 2.9g saturated fat; 27.9g carbohydrates; 9.4g sugars

Thai Vegetable Curry
with Vegetable Rice

This is such a simple recipe to make, although you could make it even easier by using a shop-bought Thai curry paste.

PREPARATION TIME: 15 minutes
COOKING TIME: 20 minutes
SERVES 4

1 tbsp coconut oil or olive oil
400g firm tofu, cut into 1cm cubes
4 spring onions, sliced
½ butternut squash (300g), peeled and cut into chunks (or use a bag of prepared squash)
1 red pepper, cut into chunks
200g green beans, halved
1 x 400ml tin coconut milk
Large handful of chopped kale or spinach
Handful of coriander leaves, to serve

For the curry paste (or use 1–2 tbsp shop-bought curry paste)
1 stick of lemongrass
2 spring onions
1 fresh green chilli, deseeded
2 garlic cloves
1cm piece of fresh ginger

Large handful of fresh coriander
1 tbsp lime juice
1 tbsp tamari soy sauce
1 tsp xylitol

For the rice
2 parsnips, chopped or 1 small cauliflower (400g), cut into
    florets
Sea salt and black pepper
2 tbsp mirin or lemon juice
1 tbsp coconut oil

First make up the curry paste – simply place all the ingredients in
a food processor or blender and blitz until combined. Add a dash
of water if needed to combine into a thick paste.

Prepare the rice. Place the parsnip or cauliflower in a food processor and process until you have fine rice-like grains. Season with
salt and pepper and add the mirin or lemon juice. Set aside while
you prepare the curry.

Heat the oil in a pan and add the tofu. Cook on each side for 5
minutes until lightly golden. Remove from the pan. Add the
spring onions, butternut squash, red pepper and green beans
and coat in the oil.

Add the curry paste and coconut milk to the pan. Simmer,
covered, for 15 minutes or until the butternut squash is just
tender. Take off the lid and add the kale or spinach and simmer
for a couple of minutes to thicken the sauce.

Just before the curry is ready heat a separate large frying pan and add the coconut oil. Add the parsnip or cauliflower rice and sauté for 2–3 minutes until soft. Spoon the vegetable rice into bowls and top with the curry. Scatter over the coriander leaves to serve.

Per serving: 218 kcal; 13.1g protein; 6.2g fat; 1g saturated fat; 27.8g carbohydrates; 17.2g sugars

Pesto and Caramelised Red Onion Pizza

There's no reason to skip the pizza with this delicious lower carb recipe. Frying the onions gently with a little xylitol gives them a delicious caramelised flavour.

PREPARATION TIME: 20 minutes
COOKING TIME: 1 hour
SERVES 4

For the base
1 small cauliflower (400g), broken into florets
3 tbsp chia seeds soaked in 4 tbsp water
3 tbsp nutritional yeast flakes
1 tbsp coconut flour
30g ground almonds
1 tbsp psyllium husks
100ml water
1 garlic clove, crushed
½ tsp sea salt
½ teaspoon dried oregano

For the topping
1 tbsp coconut oil
2 small red onions, halved and thinly sliced
1 tsp xylitol

1 quantity of vegan pesto (see page 200)
100g cherry tomatoes, sliced

For the vegan Parmesan
30g cashew nuts
2 tbsp nutritional yeast flakes
½ tsp garlic salt

First make up the vegan Parmesan. Simply place all the ingredients in a food processor and pulse until a fine meal is achieved. Store in the fridge until needed – it will keep for several weeks.

To make the base place the cauliflower in a food processor and blitz to form fine rice-like grains. Microwave or lightly steam the cauliflower for 3–5 minutes or until slightly soft, then place in a clean tea towel and squeeze out all the excess water. Place the dry cauliflower into a large bowl and add the remaining ingredients, mixing well. Preheat the oven to 190°C/fan 170°C/gas mark 5 and line a baking tray with baking parchment paper and lightly oil it.

Tip the 'dough' out onto the lined baking tray and shape into a round pizza shape, about 2cm thick, pressing down firmly. Bake in the oven for 30 minutes until the top is lightly browned. Carefully flip the pizza over onto another sheet of baking parchment and return to the oven to bake for a further 10 minutes.

Meanwhile heat the coconut oil in a pan over a low–medium heat, add the onions and xylitol and sauté very gently for 10 minutes until lightly golden. Set aside.

When the base is ready, spread the vegan pesto over the surface and then top with the caramelised onions and cherry tomatoes. Return to the oven for 10 minutes until the tomatoes have softened. Scatter with vegan Parmesan before serving.

Per serving: 450 kcal; 21.5g protein; 28g fat; 6.5g saturated fat; 26.7g carbohydrates; 7.8g sugars

One Pot Spiced Vegetable Tagine

This spicy hotpot is packed with flavour and easy to throw together.
Serve with cooked quinoa or vegetable rice for a low-carb option.

PREPARATION TIME: 15 minutes
COOKING TIME: 45 minutes
SERVES 4

1 tbsp coconut oil
1 red onion, diced
2 garlic cloves, crushed
1 sweet potato (250g), cubed
1 medium aubergine, cut into chunks
1 medium courgette, halved lengthways and sliced
1 red pepper, diced
1 tsp ground coriander
1 tsp ground cumin
Pinch of ground cinnamon
1 x 400g tin chopped tomatoes
1 tbsp harissa paste
1 tsp xylitol
60g ready-to-eat dried apricots, chopped
2 x 400g tins chickpeas, rinsed and drained
150ml vegetable stock
Cauliflower rice, to serve (see page 185)
Chopped coriander leaves, to garnish

Preheat the oven to 190°C/fan 170°C/gas mark 5.

Melt the coconut oil in a large, ovenproof dish or casserole over a low–medium heat. Add the onion, garlic, sweet potato, aubergine, courgette and red pepper and sauté for 5 minutes until lightly golden.

Add the spices and stir to coat. Stir in the chopped tomatoes, harissa paste, xylitol, apricots and chickpeas. Pour in the vegetable stock, cover the casserole and place in the oven. Cook for 40 minutes, until the vegetables are tender.

A few minutes before the tagine is ready, prepare the cauliflower rice (see page 185). Spoon into bowls and then top with the tagine. Scatter over the chopped coriander and serve.

Per serving: 339 kcal; 17.1g protein; 8.9g fat; 3.4g saturated fat; 47.8g carbohydrates; 19.7g sugars

Easy Chilli Pot

This warming bowl of chilli beans is simple to prepare and will keep in the fridge for 3–4 days, making it an ideal dish when time is short. It freezes well so make a big batch and freeze in portion.

PREPARATION TIME: 10 minutes
COOKING TIME: 45 minutes
SERVES 4

1 tbsp olive oil
1 red onion, diced
1 medium courgette, sliced
1 red pepper, chopped
1 medium sweet potato, peeled and cut into cubes
4 garlic cloves, crushed
1 tsp chilli powder
1 tsp ground cumin
½ tsp cayenne pepper
2 tsp cocoa powder
2 x 400g tins chopped tomatoes
2 x 400g tin kidney beans, rinsed and drained
1 x 400g tin cannellini beans, rinsed and drained
Sea salt and black pepper
4 sliced spring onions and 1 sliced avocado, to serve

Heat the oil in a large casserole dish and add the onion, courgette, pepper, sweet potato and garlic. Cook over a low heat for 5 minutes until the onion begins to soften.

Add the spices, cocoa powder, tomatoes and beans and stir. Bring to the boil then cover and simmer for 40 minutes. Season to taste.

Spoon into bowls and top with sliced spring onions and avocado to serve.

Per serving: 381 kcal; 16.5g protein; 9.2g fat; 1.9g saturated fat; 48.1g carbohydrates; 15.3g sugars

Almond Pad Thai

This is a wonderful vegan dish – creamy yet light and nourishing. It's quick to prepare and it will keep well in a lunch box. A spiraliser is ideal for making long vegetable noodles but you can also use a swivel potato peeler. The addition of the sea vegetables helps to boost your iodine intake, supporting a healthy metabolism and thyroid function.

PREPARATION TIME: 15 minutes
COOKING TIME: 5 minutes
SERVES 2

100g frozen edamame (soybeans)
1 carrot, spiralised or julienned
3 medium courgettes, spiralised or julienned
1 red pepper, thinly sliced
1 yellow pepper, thinly sliced
Small handful of sea vegetables (soaked and drained) or 1
    sheet of nori, crumbled
Handful of mung beansprouts, alfalfa or other sprouted seeds
Handful of watercress or spinach leaves, chopped
Handful of chopped fresh coriander leaves, to serve

For the Pad Thai dressing
60g almond or peanut butter
Zest and juice of ½ lemon

1 tsp xylitol
1 garlic clove, crushed
2 tbsp tamari soy sauce
1 tsp ground cumin
Pinch of chilli flakes
2–3 tbsp water

First make up the dressing. Place all the ingredients in a blender, adding just enough water to create a thick dressing.

Place the edamame in a pan of boiling water and cook for 5 minutes until tender. Drain.

Place all the remaining ingredients for the salad in a large bowl and toss through the Pad Thai dressing. Garnish with the coriander leaves and serve.

Per serving: 362 kcal; 22.2g protein; 21.4g fat; 3.7g saturated fat; 21.5g carbohydrates; 16.1g sugars

Stuffed Peppers

Quinoa makes a great filling for red peppers so this is a great way to use up leftover cooked quinoa. Combining it with walnuts provides protein and healthy fats for this dish. This is also delicious cold with a salad, or served alongside protein such as cooked beans, lentils or tempeh.

PREPARATION TIME: 15 minutes
COOKING TIME: 40 minutes
SERVES 4

4 red peppers
1 tbsp olive oil
1 small red onion, finely chopped
2 garlic cloves, crushed
5–6 button mushrooms (100g), chopped
175ml passata
6 sun-dried tomatoes, chopped
1 tbsp balsamic vinegar
Pinch of chilli powder
1 tbsp tamari soy sauce
80g walnuts, chopped
60g cooked quinoa (30g dry weight)

Preheat the oven to 180°C/fan 160°C/gas mark 4.

Cut the red peppers in half lengthways and discard the core and seeds. Place on a baking tray, cut side down, and bake in the oven for 10 minutes to soften them slightly. Remove from the oven and allow to cool, then turn cut side up.

Heat the oil in a frying pan and sauté the onion and garlic over a medium heat until soft. Add the mushrooms, passata, sun-dried tomatoes, vinegar, chilli powder and soy sauce and simmer for 5 minutes until the sauce has thickened slightly.

Transfer the mixture to a food processor along with the walnuts and cooked quinoa. Pulse lightly to create a chunky filling. Spoon the filling into the peppers and then bake in the oven for 20–30 minutes until the peppers are golden and soft.

Per serving: 269 kcal; 6.5g protein; 20.9g fat; 2.5g saturated fat; 13.6g carbohydrates; 9.3g sugars

Asian-Marinated Tofu Skewers with Cucumber Salad

This tangy, light and energising dish is simple to prepare – simply make up the marinade and pour over the tofu and vegetables the night before to really allow the flavours to develop. Accompany with some additional steamed vegetables. If you have any leftovers you could add them to a large mixed salad or the Creamy Caesar-style Kale Salad (see page 149) for an easy lunch option.

PREPARATION TIME: 10 minutes, plus marinating
COOKING TIME: 8 minutes
SERVES 2

400g firm tofu, drained and cut into cubes
1 red pepper, cut into chunks
½ yellow pepper, cut into chunks
6 cherry tomatoes
12 small button mushrooms
Olive oil, for griddling
6 wooden skewers, soaked in water for 30 minutes (or use metal skewers)

For the marinade
4 tbsp tamari soy sauce
½ red chilli, deseeded and chopped

2 garlic cloves, crushed
½ tsp grated fresh ginger
2 tbsp xylitol
Juice of 2 limes
1 tbsp rice wine vinegar

For the cucumber salad
1 small cucumber, peeled
1 tsp xylitol
1 tbsp rice wine vinegar
2 tbsp tamari soy sauce
1 tsp sesame oil
1 garlic clove, finely chopped
1/2 red chilli, deseeded and finely diced
2 spring onions, thinly sliced
Large handful of fresh coriander leaves

Make the marinade by whisking together all the ingredients in a small bowl, or by placing everything in a blender and whizzing until smooth.

Put the tofu, peppers, tomatoes and mushrooms in a shallow dish and pour over the marinade. Place in the fridge for at least 1 hour, or overnight.

To make the salad, slice the cucumber in half lengthways and scoop out the seeds. Slice the cucumber halves into thick diagonal chunks. Tip into a bowl and mix in all the remaining ingredients. Chill until required.

Thread the tofu cubes onto each skewer, alternating with peppers and mushrooms and adding a tomato to each skewer. Brush with the remaining marinade. Heat a little oil in a griddle pan and add the skewers. Cook for 3–4 minutes on each side until golden. Alternatively place under a hot grill, turning them during cooking so they become evenly golden. Serve with the cucumber salad.

Per serving: 305 kcal; 21.3g protein; 12.7g fat; 1.5g saturated fat; 24.1g carbohydrates; 15.4g sugars

Sweet Potato Gnocchi with Roasted Tomato Sauce

These delicious little nuggets are surprisingly easy to make and can be made in advance and kept in the fridge until ready to cook. The addition of silken tofu to the sauce is an easy way to cram in some more protein. Alternatively you can leave out the tofu and serve the gnocchi sauce with a tin of cooked mixed beans or lentils.

PREPARATION TIME: 15 minutes
COOKING TIME: 30–35 minutes
SERVES 4 as a light lunch or 2 as a main dish

200g sweet potato, peeled and cut into chunks
2 tbsp unsweetened almond milk
60g ground almonds, plus extra for dusting
½ tsp garlic salt
1 tbsp olive oil
½ tsp xanthan gum

For the roasted tomato sauce
6 tomatoes, quartered
1 red pepper, cut into chunks
½ red onion, cut in half
2 garlic cloves, chopped
1 tbsp olive oil

2 tsp balsamic vinegar
200g silken tofu
Small handful of fresh basil leaves
Sea salt and black pepper

First make the tomato sauce. Preheat the oven to 200°C/fan 180°C/ gas mark 6. Place the tomatoes, red pepper, onion and garlic on a baking tray. Drizzle over the olive oil and toss lightly to coat. Bake in the oven for 20–30 minutes until soft and golden. Remove from the oven and allow to cool slightly before placing in a food processor with the vinegar, silken tofu and basil. Whizz until smooth and thick and then transfer to a pan and keep warm. Season.

Bring a pan of water to the boil, add the sweet potato and boil for 5 minutes or until tender. Drain well. Place in a food processor with the almond milk and process until smooth. Add the remaining ingredients and pulse together to combine to make a soft dough.

Tip the dough out onto a work surface dusted with ground almonds and knead very lightly. Divide the dough into quarters and roll each piece into a long, thin log about 2cm thick. Cut the log into 3cm-long pieces and then press the top of each gnocchi with a fork to make a light indent. Put the finished gnocchi on a sheet of baking parchment while you shape the rest – you should make about 16–20 pieces.

Bring a large pan of water to the boil and add the gnocchi. Cook for about 2 minutes or until the gnocchi rise to the top of the pan. Remove with a slotted spoon and drain on kitchen paper.

Arrange the gnocchi on plates and spoon over the sauce to serve.

Per serving for 2 (*for 4): 400 (*200) kcal; 23.5g (*11.8g) protein; 17.8g (8.9g) fat; 2.1g (*1.1g) saturated fat; 33g (*16.5g) carbohydrates; 16.4g (*8.2g) sugars

Quinoa Black Bean Tacos

This is healthy fast food – the protein-packed taco filling drizzled with tangy avocado sauce makes this energising and satisfying. You can prepare the filling in advance and simply reheat when you need it.

PREPARATION TIME: 15 minutes
COOKING TIME: 15 minutes
MAKES 4 tacos (to serve 2)

1 tbsp coconut oil
1 small red onion, chopped
2 garlic cloves, crushed
½ red pepper, finely chopped
40g quinoa, rinsed and drained well
2 tbsp tomato purée
1 tsp ground cumin
½ tsp chilli powder
½ tsp smoked paprika
250ml vegetable stock
1 x 400g tin black beans or kidney beans, rinsed and drained
Sea salt and black pepper
4 corn taco shells and shredded lettuce, to serve

For the avocado dressing
½ avocado, chopped

Juice of 1 lime
½ red chilli, deseeded and chopped
1 tbsp chopped fresh coriander
Pinch of sea salt

Heat the oil in a pan and sauté the onion, garlic and red pepper over a medium heat for 2–3 minutes until soft. Add the quinoa and stir to coat in the oil. Pour over the tomato purée, spices and stock and bring to a simmer. Cover and cook for 15 minutes until the quinoa is tender. Stir in the beans to warm through and season to taste.

Make the avocado dressing by simply blending all the ingredients together in a blender. Chill in the fridge until required (it will keep for 2–3 days).

To serve, warm the taco shells following the instructions on the packet and fill with lettuce and bean filling. Drizzle over the avocado dressing and enjoy.

Per serving: 445 kcal; 15.3g protein; 19.2g fat; 5.2g saturated fat; 52.1g carbohydrates; 11.1g sugars

RECIPES
Snacks and Sides

Cauliflower Steaks

These are fabulous served with warm beans or lentils. The extra florets can be added to a salad or eaten as a snack the following day.

PREPARATION TIME: 10 minutes
COOKING TIME: 30 minutes
SERVES 2

1 small cauliflower (400g)
1 tbsp olive oil
½ tsp garlic salt
½ tsp ground cumin
Freshly ground black pepper
1 tablespoon freshly chopped parsley, to garnish

Preheat the oven to 190°C/fan 170°C/gas mark 5.

Place the cauliflower on the cutting board and working from the centre, slice the head into 2cm thick 'steaks'. Cut the end pieces into little florets.

Mix together the oil and spices and season with pepper. Toss the florets in 1 teaspoon of the olive oil spice mixture and arrange on one side of a lined or greased baking tray. Place the cauliflower steaks on the baking tray and brush with the remaining oil.

Roast in the oven for 15 minutes, then flip the steaks over and roast for another 15 minutes. The steaks are done when they're browned on the outside and tender on the inside. The florets will be crispy – if they cook too quickly remove them from the oven before the steaks. Sprinkle with chopped parsley and serve hot or cold.

Per serving: 109 kcal; 7.4g protein; 6.5g fat; 1.1g saturated fat; 5.6g carbohydrates; 4.8g sugars

Red Cabbage and Apple Sauerkraut

Real fermented sauerkraut (not the stuff on the supermarket shelf) is simple to make and great for improving digestion. It's also low in calories yet filling, making it ideal for weight loss. You can further improve the probiotic content by using a vegetable starter kit, which are readily available from online suppliers.

PREPARATION TIME: 15 minutes
FERMENTING TIME: 10–14 days
MAKES 1 large Kilner jar

½ red cabbage (300g)
2 carrots, grated
1 tsp grated fresh ginger
1 tbsp caraway seeds
1 tbsp fennel seeds
2 apples, cored and chopped
2 tsp sea salt
Vegetable culture starter kit (optional)

Sterilise a 2 litre (3½ pint) Kilner jar: you can either do this by placing them in a dishwasher or wash them in hot, soapy water, rinse well and place in a low oven to dry out completely.

Shred the cabbage and carrots in a food processor, then place in a large glass or stainless steel bowl. Stir in the ginger, seeds and apple.

Dissolve the sea salt in 150ml water and add the vegetable culture starter, if using, following the instructions on the packet. Pour this over the vegetable mixture and use your hands to massage it into the vegetables.

Fill the sterilised jar with the cabbage mixture, pressing down firmly to leave a little gap at the top. The cabbage should be completely submerged in the liquid, so add more water if necessary. Seal the jar and leave at room temperature away from sunlight for at least 10 days but up to 2 weeks. Taste the sauerkraut – it should be tangy. Store in the fridge with the lid on for up to 1 month.

Per 100g serving: 26kcal; 1.1g protein; 0.6g fat; 0g saturated fat; 5.3g carbohydrates; 5.1g sugars

Creamy Celeriac Slaw

A delicious creamy accompaniment to salads, falafels and burgers. Using coconut yoghurt also adds some beneficial bacteria to support digestive health. High in fibre, this makes a satisfying and healthy snack too.

PREPARATION TIME: 10 minutes
SERVES 4

¼ celeriac (250g), shredded
1 large carrot, grated
2 tbsp capers, chopped
1 tsp Dijon mustard
2 tbsp red wine vinegar
4 tbsp coconut yoghurt, shop-bought or homemade (see page 81)
Handful of fresh parsley, chopped
Sea salt and black pepper

Place the celeriac and carrot in a large bowl. Mix the remaining ingredients together and stir into the vegetables. Taste and adjust the seasoning.

Keep in the fridge for 2–3 days.

Per 130g serving: 31 kcal; 1.2g protein; 0.5g fat; 0.1g saturated fat; 5g carbohydrates; 4.6g sugars

Creamy Nacho Dip

A deliciously creamy-tasting dip that makes a great alternative to hummus or cheesy dips. Try this as a snack with vegetable sticks or spread onto flaxseed crackers (see page 258). This will keep in the fridge for 4–5 days and can also be frozen.

PREPARATION TIME: 10 minutes
COOKING TIME: 10 minutes
SERVES 16

200g cauliflower florets
200g carrots, diced
1 tbsp olive oil
1 small onion, diced
1/2 tsp ground cumin
½ tsp garlic powder
½ tsp barbecue seasoning
½ tsp smoked paprika
Juice of ½ lemon
4 tbsp nutritional yeast flakes
1 tsp tomato purée
Sea salt and black pepper

Bring a pan of water to the boil and add the cauliflower and carrots. Cook until soft, about 8 minutes. Drain well, reserving the cooking liquid.

Meanwhile heat the oil in a pan and sauté the onion over a medium heat for 2–3 minutes or until soft.

Place all the ingredients in a food processor or blender and blitz until smooth. Add a little of the reserved cooking liquid if needed to make a thick dip.

Per 30g serving: 20 kcal; 1.2g protein; 0.8g fat; 0.1g saturated fat; 2g carbohydrates; 1.4g sugars

Roasted Root Hummus

This is a fabulous way to use up leftover roasted vegetables. If you are cooking from scratch simply toss the vegetables in a little olive oil and roast for 20–30 minutes until tender. Delicious served with vegetable sticks.

PREPARATION TIME: 10 minutes
SERVES 14

1 x 400g tin chickpeas, rinsed and drained
150g roasted root vegetables, such as carrots, celeriac or
   parsnips
Juice of 1 lemon
2 tbsp tahini paste
1 garlic clove, crushed
½ tsp ground cumin
Pinch of cayenne pepper
Sea salt and black pepper

Place all the ingredients in a food processor and blitz until smooth. If needed add a little water to help bind the hummus together into a thick, smooth dip.

Chill in the fridge until needed – it will keep in the fridge for 3–4 days.

Per 30g serving: 35 kcal; 1.6g protein; 1.7g fat; 0.2g saturated fat; 3.2g carbohydrates; 0.8g sugars

Spiced Crunchy Chickpeas

A fabulous protein snack – so much healthier than a bowl of popcorn. Using tinned chickpeas makes this a quick and easy store cupboard recipe. Make up a double batch as these will keep in an airtight container for 4–5 days – they are great for sprinkling over salads for a protein boost.

PREPARATION TIME: 5 minutes
COOKING TIME: 20 minutes
SERVES 8

1 x 400g tin chickpeas, rinsed and drained
½ tsp onion salt
½ tsp garlic powder
½ tsp smoked paprika
¼ tsp cayenne pepper
1 tsp olive oil

Preheat the oven to 200°C/fan 180°C/gas mark 6.

Tip the chickpeas onto a clean tea towel and rub lightly to dry, then place them in a bowl and sprinkle over the spices and oil. Toss lightly to combine.

Spread the chickpeas out on a baking tray and bake in the oven for 20 minutes or until golden and crisp. Allow to cool then store in an airtight container.

Per (30g) serving: 38 kcal; 2.1g protein; 1.3g fat; 0.1g saturated fat; 4.5g carbohydrates; 0.1g sugars

Roasted Red Pepper and Bean Dip

This is an easy store cupboard dip or spread that takes just minutes to prepare. Rich in antioxidants and essential fats this is fabulously healthy. Using a jar of roasted red peppers keeps this hassle free.

PREPARATION TIME: 5 minutes
SERVES 18

½ tsp smoked paprika
1 garlic clove, crushed
1 x 400g tin cannellini beans, rinsed and drained
225g roasted red peppers from a jar
3 tbsp flaxseed oil, walnut oil or olive oil
1 tbsp balsamic vinegar
1 tsp xylitol
Sea salt and black pepper

Simply place everything in a food processor or blender and blitz until smooth and creamy. Season to taste.

This will keep in the fridge for 3–4 days.

Per (30g) serving: 38 kcal; 1g protein; 2.5g fat; 0.2g saturated fat; 2.7g carbohydrates; 0.9g sugars

Buffalo Cauliflower and Broccoli Bites

These make a brilliant healthy snack – crisp and tangy and delicious served on their own or dipped into a red pepper dip or tango mayo (see pages 247 and 85).

PREPARATION TIME: 10 minutes
COOKING TIME: 35 minutes
SERVES 10

400g cauliflower or broccoli florets
60g gram (chickpea) flour or coconut flour
1 tsp garlic powder
1 tsp onion salt
60ml water
60ml hot sauce, preferably sugar-free

Preheat the oven to 220°C/fan 200°/gas mark 7 and line a baking tray with non-stick baking parchment.

Mix together the gram (chickpea) flour, garlic powder, onion salt and water and mix to form a thick batter. Dip each floret into the batter so that it is fully coated and place on the lined baking tray.

Bake in the oven for 15 minutes, then drizzle over the hot sauce, making sure all the florets are coated. Return to the oven and bake for a further 20 minutes until crispy.

Per 60g serving: 38 kcal; 2.7g protein; 0.7g fat; 0.1g saturated fat; 5g carbohydrates; 2.1g sugars

Sweet Potato Crisps

Light and crunchy these are delicious as a snack or served with a dip. If possible use a mandoline to create very thin slices. As an alternative you could make sweet potato shoe strings by spiralising the sweet potato.

PREPARATION TIME: 10 minutes
COOKING TIME: 20 minutes
SERVES 5–6

1 medium sweet potato (300g)
1 tsp barbecue seasoning
1 tsp ground cumin
1 tsp cornflour
1 tbsp olive oil
Sea salt and black pepper

Preheat the oven to 200°C/fan 180°C/gas mark 6 and line a baking tray with non-stick baking parchment.

Peel the sweet potato and slice thinly, using either a mandoline or very sharp knife. Place the slices in a large bowl and toss with the barbecue seasoning, cumin and cornflour. Drizzle over the olive oil and toss again. Season with salt and pepper.

Place the sweet potato chips in a single layer on the lined baking tray. Bake in the oven for 10 minutes, then flip the chips over and bake for another 5–10 minutes, watching them carefully so that they don't turn too brown. Remove from the oven and place on kitchen paper to drain and cool.

Per 60g serving: 69 kcal; 0.9g protein; 2g fat; 0.3g saturated fat; 12g carbohydrates; 3g sugars

Pecan Nut and Pumpkin Butter

This is a delicious sweet treat that can be spread on sliced apple, oatcakes or crackers. Using tinned pumpkin purée makes this an easy recipe to prepare.

PREPARATION TIME: 10 minutes
COOKING TIME: 13 minutes
MAKES 20 servings

100g pecan nuts
1 x 400g tin pumpkin purée
1 apple, chopped
1 tbsp lemon juice
2 tbsp xylitol
1 tsp ground cinnamon
½ tsp ground nutmeg
1 tbsp vanilla extract

Place the pecan nuts in a dry frying pan and toast lightly over a medium heat for 2–3 minutes, shaking the pan occasionally. Set aside.

Place all the remaining ingredients (except the nuts) in a pan and add a splash of water. Cover and simmer gently for 10 minutes until the apple is very soft. Set aside to cool.

Place the contents of the pan and the toasted nuts in a food processor and blitz until completely smooth. Spoon into a clean jar or container and store in the fridge until needed (it will keep for 1 week).

Per 30g serving: 42 kcal; 0.6g protein; 3.6g fat; 0.3g saturated fat; 2.5g carbohydrates; 0.9g sugars

Cinnamon Trail Mix

A delicious toasted trail mix, which makes an ideal snack on the go. You can vary the nuts according to what you have available. Make up a batch and keep in an airtight container.

PREPARATION TIME: 10 minutes
COOKING TIME: 18 minutes
MAKES 10 servings

1 tbsp coconut oil
1 tsp xylitol
½ tsp ground cinnamon
Pinch of sea salt
1 tbsp vanilla extract
60g walnut pieces
60g almonds
60g pecan nuts
100g mixed seeds (sunflower, pumpkin, hemp etc.)

Preheat the oven to 180°C/fan 160°C/gas mark 4 and line a baking tray with non-stick baking parchment.

Place the coconut oil and xylitol in a pan and place over a low heat to melt the coconut oil. Stir in the cinnamon, salt and vanilla. Add the nuts and seeds and stir to coat.

Spread out on the lined baking sheet and bake in the oven for 10–15 minutes, stirring occasionally, until they turn golden.

Allow to cool then transfer to an airtight container (it will keep for at least 1 week).

Per 30g serving: 186 kcal; 5.3g protein; 17.2g fat; 2.4g saturated fat; 2.7g carbohydrates; 0.7g sugars

Pizza Kale Crisps

This is a fabulous way to eat more kale! These crisps are amazing and very addictive, as well as being simple to prepare. Don't worry if you don't have a dehydrator – you can easily bake these in the oven instead. Make up a big batch as it will go quickly!

PREPARATION TIME: 10 minutes
COOKING TIME: 20 minutes or 10–11 hours in a dehydrator
MAKES 8 servings

1 tomato
3 tbsp tamari soy sauce
2 tbsp apple cider vinegar
2 tbsp nutritional yeast flakes
1 tsp smoked paprika
1 tsp ground cumin
1 tsp garlic salt
Pinch of chilli flakes
10 sun-dried tomatoes
½ red pepper, chopped
30g soft dates
2 tbsp water
200g chopped kale

Blend all the ingredients except the kale in a high-speed blender until completely smooth.

Put the chopped kale in a bowl and add the blended sauce. Thoroughly combine until the kale is completely coated.

If using a dehydrator scatter the kale on a non-stick dehydrator sheet in a way that will allow air to circulate around it. Dehydrate at 48°C for around 10 hours. Remove from the non-stick sheet, transfer to a mesh sheet and continue dehydrating for another 1 hour or until the kale is completely dry.

Alternatively preheat the oven to 180°C/fan 160°C/gas mark 4 and line a baking tray with a non-stick silicone baking mat. Spread the kale pieces on the lined baking tray and bake in the oven for 10–20 minutes, turning occasionally until the kale is crisp.

Per 60g serving: 59 kcal; 2.5g protein; 3.8g fat; 0.5g saturated fat; 3.7g carbohydrates; 2.7g sugars

Flaxseed and Chia Seed Crackers

You can make a whole range of different flavoured crackers using this recipe – try replacing the red pepper with a handful of black olives or some finely chopped herbs. If you want to increase the overall protein content simply add a scoop of protein powder.

PREPARATION TIME: 15 minutes
COOKING TIME: 1½ hours or 12 hours in a dehydrator
MAKES 16 crackers

250g whole flaxseed
30g chia seeds
30g plain protein powder
1 red pepper
4 sun-dried tomatoes
100g cherry tomatoes
Juice of 1 lemon
½ tsp garlic salt

Simply place all the ingredients into a food processor and blend to form a stiff paste. You may need to add a little water if it is too dry. It should form a sticky dough.

Use a spatula to spread the mixture onto dehydrator sheets and then mark out cracker shapes with a knife. Dehydrate at 46–48°C for around 9 hours, or overnight, until they are dry. Flip them over and continue to dehydrate for a further 3 hours until they are crisp.

Alternatively preheat the oven to 150°C/fan 130°C/gas mark 2 and line a baking tray with a non-stick silicone baking mat. Spread the mixture onto the lined baking tray and mark into crackers as above. Bake in the oven for 1 hour, then flip the crackers over and cook for a further 20–30 minutes until crisp.

Per cracker: 109 kcal; 4.7g protein; 8g fat; 0.8g saturated fat; 6.4g carbohydrates; 1.2g sugars

Chocolate Buckwheat Nibbles

A wonderful sweet chocolate treat – ideal as a snack or for breakfast with some fruit and coconut yoghurt. The addition of chocolate protein powder is a great way to boost the protein content. Soaking the buckwheat overnight 'activates' the grains, making them easier to digest – just make sure you drain thoroughly before using. Lucuma is a popular 'superfood' powder that has a natural sweetness and caramel flavour. It is available online and from health food stores.

PREPARATION TIME: 10 minutes, plus overnight soaking
COOKING TIME: 40 minutes
MAKES 10 servings

160g buckwheat, soaked overnight
2 tbsp coconut oil
1 tbsp tahini paste
30g desiccated coconut
1 tbsp cocoa powder
2 tbsp xylitol
1 tbsp lucuma powder (optional)
30g chocolate protein powder
½ tsp ground cinnamon

Preheat the oven to 190°C/fan 170°C/gas mark 5 and line a baking tray with baking parchment.

Rinse and drain the buckwheat thoroughly.

Put the coconut oil and tahini into a large pan and melt over a low heat. Remove from the heat and stir in the remaining ingredients, including the drained buckwheat. Spread the mixture out onto the lined baking tray.

Bake in the oven for 30–40 minutes, stirring occasionally, until the buckwheat is crunchy. Allow to cool and then store in an airtight container for 1–2 weeks.

Per 30g serving: 129 kcal; 4.3g protein; 5.2g fat; 3.4g saturated fat; 17.8g carbohydrates; 0.9g sugars

Feel Good Treats

Chocolate Orange Pots

This is a delicious, rich recipe that is naturally sweetened with orange. Using the orange naturally sweetens this recipe without the need for syrups. If you want to boost the protein content, swap one of the tablespoons of cocoa powder with chocolate protein powder.

PREPARATION TIME: 10 minutes
COOKING TIME: 2 minutes
SERVES 4

100g sugar-free and dairy-free dark chocolate, melted
1 tbsp unsweetened almond milk
2 tbsp cocoa powder (or 1 tbsp cocoa powder and 1 tbsp chocolate protein powder)
1 large orange, peeled and pips removed
250g silken tofu, drained
Grated orange zest, to decorate (optional)

Place the chocolate and almond milk in a pan and gently melt over a low heat, stirring to combine.

Put the melted chocolate into a food processor or blender with all the remaining ingredients and blend until smooth and creamy. Spoon into four ramekins and decorate with a little orange zest, if wished.

This can be frozen for up to 1 month or will keep in the fridge for 3–4 days.

Per serving: 228 kcal; 12.6g protein; 15.4g fat; 7.2g saturated fat; 11.4g carbohydrates; 4.5g sugars

Baked Plums with Spices

Roasting the plums gives them plenty of flavour and creates a delicious, healthy sweet treat. Serve these with nut cream or coconut yoghurt (see pages 83 and 81) as a light breakfast or snack.

PREPARATION TIME: 5 minutes
COOKING TIME: 30 minutes
SERVES 4

8 plums
250ml red grape juice
2 cinnamon sticks
½ tsp ground cinnamon
4 star anise

Preheat the oven to 180°C/fan 160°C/gas mark 4.

Arrange the plums in a single layer in a shallow baking dish. Pour over the grape juice and add the spices.

Bake for 30 minutes until the fruit is soft but not quite collapsed. Serve warm or cold with nut cream or coconut yoghurt, if wished.

Per serving: 50 kcal; 0.6g protein; 0.1g fat; 0g saturated fat; 12.6g carbohydrates; 12g sugars

Layered Berry, Yoghurt and Granola Pots

This versatile dessert can be easily adapted to include other fruits, such as chopped apple or baked plums. Instead of granola you could simply use a selection of nuts and seeds or try the Chocolate Buckwheat Nibbles (see page 260).

PREPARATION TIME: 5 minutes
SERVES 1

50g Nutty Pear Granola Clusters (see page 103)
100g coconut yoghurt, shop-bought or homemade (see page 81)
50g mixed berries (fresh or frozen)

Simply layer the granola, yoghurt and berries in a bowl or glass.

You can store this prepared in the fridge for up to 2 days.

Per serving: 240 kcal; 8.1g protein; 15g fat; 3.3g saturated fat; 18.5g carbohydrates; 11.6g sugars

Mango Lime Sorbet

This is such a simple recipe, needing only four ingredients. If you have a high-speed blender or food processor you can make instant sorbet by using frozen mango chunks. If not, simply blend the ingredients and freeze until firm. You can boost your protein intake by adding a couple of scoops of vanilla protein powder too.

PREPARATION TIME: 5 minutes
SERVES 4

5 fresh mint leaves
2 tbsp lime juice
4 tbsp orange juice
400g frozen mango chunks
2 scoops (60g) vanilla protein powder (optional)

Place the mint leaves, lime juice, orange juice and protein powder, if using, in a high-speed blender or food processor and blend until smooth.

Add the frozen mango chunks and process on high speed to create a thick, instant sorbet. You may have to stop and scrape down the sides as you blend.

Eat immediately or spoon into a container and freeze until required.

Per serving (*without protein powder): 107 (*50) kcal; 12.1g (*0.6g) protein; 1.3g (*0.2g) fat; 0.1g (*0.1g) saturated fat; 14g (*11.2g) carbohydrates; 8.2g (*6g) sugars

Choc Chip Mint Protein Ice Cream

A lovely creamy recipe – perfect for satisfying cravings. The added protein boost from the protein powder will help to stabilise blood sugar levels, making this the ideal snack. The green superfood powder is optional (try wheatgrass or spirulina powder) but gives the ice cream a lovely light-green colour.

PREPARATION TIME: 10 minutes, plus freezing
SERVES 6

1 x 400ml tin full-fat coconut milk
5 fresh mint leaves
50g xylitol or 1 tsp granulated stevia, to taste
2 scoops (60g) vanilla protein powder
½ avocado, chopped
1 tsp peppermint extract
1 tbsp coconut oil, melted
1 tsp green superfood powder (optional)
60g dairy-free and sugar-free chocolate chips

Place all the ingredients except the chocolate chips into a high-speed blender and process until smooth and creamy.

Pour the mixture into an ice cream maker and churn according to the manufacturer's instructions. (Alternatively you can make this without a machine by pouring into a shallow container and placing in the freezer for 4 hours, stirring with a fork every hour to break up the ice crystals.)

Once it starts to become firm add the chocolate chips. Eat immediately or spoon into a container and freeze until needed.

Per serving: 159 kcal; 9.5g protein; 8.7g fat; 4.4g saturated fat; 16.1g carbohydrates; 4.8g sugars

Protein Banana Ice Cream

This is such a quick healthy recipe using just three ingredients – it's ideal if you need to use up some ripe bananas (a good tip is to peel and chop ripe bananas and freeze them in containers or bags, ready to use for smoothies or recipes like this one). You can vary the flavours too – try adding a little coffee powder for a mocha version, or stir in some chocolate chips or nuts.

PREPARATION TIME: 10 minutes, plus freezing
SERVES 4

4 ripe bananas
1 scoop (30g) chocolate protein powder
1 tbsp cocoa powder

Peel the bananas and cut them into small pieces. Place on a baking tray lined with baking parchment and freeze for 3–4 hours until firm.

Put the frozen bananas into a food processor or blender and pulse until smooth. You may need to stop and scrape down the sides as you blend. When the mixture is smooth, add the protein powder and cocoa powder and blend again until completely incorporated. Serve immediately or spoon into a container and freeze until required.

Per serving: 131 kcal; 7.4g protein; 1.4g fat; 0.4g saturated fat; 23.3g carbohydrates; 21g sugars

Superberry Protein Balls

These are a popular snack with my children and are also a great energising boost before or after a workout – perfect as an after-noon pick-me-up or when you fancy a sweet treat. Make a batch of these and store in the fridge or freezer.

PREPARATION TIME: 10 minutes, plus chilling
COOKING TIME 2 minutes
MAKES 20 balls

2 tbsp coconut oil, melted
3 tbsp xylitol or 1–2 tsp granulated stevia
220g nut butter (cashew, almond or peanut)
4 tbsp coconut flour
60g vanilla or berry protein powder
1 tsp acai or goji berry powder (optional)
50g dried berries (cranberries, cherries etc.)
Desiccated coconut, to coat

Place the coconut oil and xylitol (or stevia) in a pan. Gently melt over a low heat, stirring to dissolve the xylitol. Allow to cool slightly and then tip into a food processor and add the nut butter. Process briefly until combined.

Add the coconut flour, protein powder and acai or goji berry powder, if using, and blend again to form a stiff dough. If it seems too wet add a little more coconut flour or protein powder. The mixture should be firm but soft. Add the dried berries and pulse briefly, just to break them up slightly.

Tip some desiccated coconut onto a plate. Take small spoonfuls of the mixture and roll into walnut-sized balls, then roll them in the coconut until coated on all sides.

Chill in the fridge for about 30 minutes to firm up before eating. Transfer to an airtight container and store in the fridge for up to 5 days or freeze for up to 1 month.

Per ball: 117 kcal; 5.5g protein; 8g fat; 2.8g saturated fat; 7g carbohydrates; 2.5g sugars

Vegan Protein Chocolate Brownies

These are so simple to make and a great way to use up ripe bananas. You can also freeze these brownies for up to 3 months.

PREPARATION TIME: 10 minutes
COOKING TIME: 30 minutes
MAKES 16 brownies

3 medium ripe bananas
120g almond nut butter or other nut butter
30g cocoa powder
1 tbsp baking powder
½ tsp bicarbonate of soda
1 tbsp vanilla extract
80g chocolate protein powder
2 tbsp unsweetened almond milk or soya milk
60g dairy-free and sugar-free chocolate chips

Preheat the oven to 180°C/fan 160°C/gas mark 4 and grease and line a 20cm square traybake tin with baking parchment.

Place all the ingredients except the chocolate chips in a food processor and blend until smooth. Stir in the chocolate chips, reserving a few for the top. Spoon the mixture into the prepared tin and scatter over the remaining chocolate chips.

Bake in the oven for 20–30 minutes until cooked through and a skewer inserted into the centre comes out clean. Remove from the oven and allow to cool completely in the tin before cutting into squares.

Per serving: 110 kcal; 6.3g protein; 6.3g fat; 2g saturated fat; 8.7g carbohydrates; 4.5g sugars

Apricot Chia Energy Balls

These are the perfect pick-me-up snack. Naturally sweetened with dried apricots, the chia seeds add Omega-3 fats, protein and fibre to keep your energy levels soaring. If you want a protein boost replace half the almonds with protein powder.

PREPARATION TIME: 10 minutes, plus chilling
MAKES 12 balls

60g dried apricots, chopped
1 tbsp nut butter
50g coconut oil, melted
60g desiccated coconut, plus extra for rolling
60g ground almonds
3 tbsp chia seeds
Pinch of sea salt

Place the apricots, nut butter and coconut oil in a food processor and blend to form a thick paste. Add the remaining ingredients and blend until the mixture comes together to form a soft dough.

Take small spoonfuls of the mixture and roll into walnut-sized balls. Place the desiccated coconut on a plate and roll the balls in it until they are well coated. Place in the fridge for at least 30 minutes to firm up.

These will keep in the fridge in an airtight container for up to 5 days.

Per ball: 134 kcal; 2.5g protein; 11.9g fat; 6.7g saturated fat; 4.4g carbohydrates; 2.6g sugars

Raspberry Almond Muffins

Baked treats such as muffins are one of the things my vegan clients miss the most so I have created this recipe with them in mind – and my son likes to snack on them too. The use of psyllium husks is a great egg alternative and helps to bind the muffin. I like to use frozen raspberries for convenience but you could use fresh if they are in season.

PREPARATION TIME: 15 minutes
COOKING TIME: 40 minutes
MAKES 6 large muffins

1 tbsp psyllium husks
200ml unsweetened almond milk
30g hazelnuts
110g ground almonds
20g desiccated coconut
2 tsp baking powder
30g xylitol
½ tsp pure vanilla extract
2 tbsp coconut oil, melted
150g frozen or fresh raspberries
60g dairy-free and sugar-free chocolate chips or dried berries

Whisk the psyllium husks and almond milk together in a large mixing bowl and then set aside, allowing the mixture to thicken.

Pulse the hazelnuts in a food processor until you have a fine powder. Add the ground almonds, coconut, baking powder and xylitol and pulse again to combine.

Pour in the almond milk mixture, the vanilla and coconut oil and process briefly, then allow the mixture to sit for 10 minutes. Meanwhile preheat the oven to 180°C/fan 160°C/gas mark 4 and line a large 6-hole muffin tray with paper cases.

Fold the raspberries into the batter, along with the chocolate chips or dried berries. Pour the batter into the muffin cases and bake for 40 minutes or until the muffins have firmed up and turned golden brown. They are cooked when a skewer or cocktail stick inserted into the middle comes out clean. Allow to cool in the tin for 10 minutes before removing.

Per muffin: 284 kcal; 6.7g protein; 23.6g fat; 8g saturated fat; 12.3g carbohydrates; 2.5g sugars

Apple Flapjacks

A simple no-bake recipe that is low in sugar, thanks to the addition of apple purée (I use pots of baby apple sauce for ease). If you can't get puffed rice use chopped nuts or desiccated coconut instead.

PREPARATION TIME: 10 minutes, plus freezing
MAKE 12 slices

50g pecan nuts, finely chopped
25g puffed rice (no added sugar)
100g gluten-free oats, quinoa flakes or buckwheat flakes
45g mixed seeds (sunflower, sesame, pumpkin)
40g dried berries or dried apple pieces, chopped
65g cashew nut butter or other nut butter (no added sugar)
40g coconut oil
100g organic apple purée

Line a 20cm square tin with baking parchment.

Place all the dry ingredients in a large bowl and mix with a spoon. Meanwhile put the nut butter and coconut oil into a small pan and melt gently over a low heat, stirring to combine. Pour into the bowl of dry ingredients along with the apple purée and mix well.

Spoon the mixture into the prepared tin and press down firmly to make sure it sticks together. Place in the freezer for 30 minutes to firm up, then turn out and cut into bars or squares. Store in the fridge in an airtight container for 1–2 weeks or freeze for up to 1 month.

Per slice: 166 kcal; 3.4g protein; 11.5g fat; 3.9g saturated fat; 12.5g carbohydrates; 4g sugars

Teff Chocolate Bread

Teff is a nutritious protein-rich gluten-free grain that is becoming more readily available in good supermarkets and from online suppliers. This is a fabulous recipe for a healthy carb fix and is delicious served with a little nut butter – perfect for breakfast or as a pick-me-up snack. It freezes well; simply slice and freeze in plastic food bags.

PREPARATION TIME: 15 minutes
COOKING TIME: 50–55 minutes
MAKES 1 loaf (10 slices)

100g chopped pitted dates
125ml boiling water
1 banana
50g coconut oil, melted
200g teff flour
30g cocoa powder
2 tbsp psyllium husks
1 tsp ground cinnamon
1 tsp bicarbonate of soda
1 tsp baking powder
¼ tsp fine sea salt
1 tbsp lemon juice
1 tbsp ground flaxseed or chia seeds, soaked in 3 tbsp water
   for 5 minutes

Place the dates in a bowl and pour over the boiling water; leave to soak for 15 minutes. Meanwhile preheat the oven to 180°C/fan 160°C/gas mark 4 and grease and line a 900g loaf tin with baking parchment.

Place the dates and the soaking liquid in a food processor with the banana and coconut oil and process to form a sticky paste. Add all the remaining ingredients and process to combine to a thick batter.

Spoon the batter into the loaf tin and bake for 50–55 minutes or until a skewer inserted into the loaf comes out clean. Remove from oven and allow to cool in the tin for about 10 minutes before turning out onto a wire rack to cool completely.

Per slice: 165 kcal; 3.6g protein; 6.7g fat; 4.8g saturated fat; 19.9g carbohydrates; 8.5g sugars

Protein Berry Mug Cake

Feel the need for cake? Then try this instant recipe. It's quick and easy to make, tastes amazing and is healthy enough to have for breakfast. If you don't have a microwave you can spoon into a small ovenproof dish and bake instead.

PREPARATION TIME: 5 minutes
COOKING TIME: 2 minutes (microwave) or 20 minutes (oven)
MAKES 1 mug cake

1 tbsp ground flaxseed or chia seeds, or 3 tbsp aquafaba (see page 49)
1 tbsp coconut flour
1 scoop (30g) vanilla or berry protein powder
1 tbsp xylitol or ½ tsp granulated stevia
½ tsp baking powder
1 tsp ground cinnamon
3 tbsp apple purée (from a jar) or ½ mashed banana
2 tbsp unsweetened almond milk
30g frozen blueberries

Place the flaxseed or chia seeds in a small bowl with 3 tbsp water and allow to soak for 5 minutes.

In a mug combine the coconut flour, protein powder, xylitol or stevia, baking powder and cinnamon. Beat in the flaxseed mixture, apple purée or banana and almond milk. Fold in the blueberries.

Microwave for 1–2 minutes depending on the power of your microwave until the cake has risen and is cooked through. It should be soft inside. Alternatively spoon into a small baking dish or a couple of ramekins and bake in an oven preheated to 180°C/ fan 160°C/gas mark 4 for 15–20 minutes. Eat warm, straight from the mug!

Per serving: 349 kcal; 28.1g protein; 10.9g fat; 2.7g saturated fat; 45.9g carbohydrates; 15.4g sugars

Q & A

I have a lot of weight to lose. Can I follow this plan for longer than 30 days?

Absolutely. The diet is suitable for following long term. Once you have completed the 30 days you can either restart the plan outlined or pick and choose your meal options from the recipes.

I find beans difficult to digest – is there an alternative?

Not everyone finds beans easy to digest. Experiment with different varieties as you may find some easier to tolerate than others. Always make sure you use properly cooked beans that have been rinsed thoroughly. If they are problematic for you try lentils, especially red split lentils, which tend to be easier to digest. You may also find soy products like tofu and tempeh are less likely to cause problems.

I have a family – can the rest of my family follow the plan?

There is no reason why the rest of your family cannot follow a vegan diet. If they don't want to lose weight, they may require larger portions or slightly more starch or snacks from the plan.

Can I swap around the recipes?

Yes. For example, if you can't take soup to work have the soup meals in the evening and eat the dinner option at lunchtime. If there are some recipes you love, there is no reason why you cannot eat them more frequently but always aim to include plenty of variety each day.

Can I eat my snack in the evening?

As mentioned, snacks are optional – only include them if you are really hungry. There is no reason why you cannot save your snack and eat it later in the day if you need it. However, avoid late-night snacking as it can interfere with digestion which will affect sleep.

Shopping Lists

As explained in the *Go Lean Vegan* Pantry chapter on pages 39–51, it is a good idea to keep a well-stocked cupboard so that you always have a good supply of healthy oils, seasonings, nuts and nut butters, dried pulses and tinned goods to hand. The following shopping lists will help you plan what fresh produce and additional items you will need for the weeks ahead.

WEEK 1

Seasonings

Tamari soy sauce

Cayenne pepper

Ground cinnamon

Ground cumin

Dried oregano

Garlic salt

Onion salt

Garlic powder

Smoked paprika

Cumin seeds

Cinnamon sticks

Chilli flakes

Olive oil

Dijon mustard

Flaxseed oil or Omega blend oil

Nutritional yeast flakes

Tomato purée

Vegan bouillon powder

Coconut oil

Apple cider vinegar

Bag of mixed sea vegetables or flakes

Vanilla and chocolate protein powders

Pantry

Tahini paste

Almond nut butter

Peanut butter (no added sugar or salt)

Chickpea (gram) flour

Cashew nuts (260g)

Silken UHT tofu (600g)

Sugar-free vegan chocolate (100g)

Red split lentils (75g)

Buckwheat (160g)

Psyllium husks (15g)

Chia seeds

Cocoa powder

Vanilla extract

Spirulina powder (optional)

Matcha green tea powder or green tea bags

Xylitol

Gluten-free oats (15g)

Coconut flour

Pistachio nuts (60g)

Ground almonds (30g)

Chopped tomatoes (1 x 400g tin)

Chickpeas (3 x 400g tins)

Cannellini beans (3 x 400g tins)

Mixed beans (1 x 400g tin)

Butterbeans (1 x 400g tin)

Coconut milk (1 x 400ml tin)

Shelled hemp seeds or mixed seeds

Mixed nuts (1 bag)

Fresh fruit and vegetables

Kiwi fruit (1)

Pear (1)

Fresh ginger

Watermelon, fresh or frozen (100g)

Small bananas (2)

Orange (3)

Baby Spinach (200g)

Watercress (1 bag)

Carrots (3)

Avocado (1)

Bags of mixed salad (5)

Lemons (8)

Aubergine (1)

Cauliflowers (2)

Courgettes (4)

Sweet potato (300g)

Celery (1 head)

Broccoli (300g)

Garlic bulbs (2)

Red peppers (2)

Yellow pepper (1)

Onions (2)

Red onion (1)

Alfalfa or mung bean sprouts
(small packet)

Pomegranate (1) or 30g pomegranate seeds

Raw Sauerkraut (or use
homemade)

Fresh herbs (mint, basil,
coriander,

Apple (1)

Cucumbers (2)

Tomatoes (6)

Cherry tomatoes (200g)

Kale (200g)

Fridge and freezer

Coconut yoghurt (or use
homemade, 400g)

Frozen mixed berries (100g)

Frozen broccoli florets

Frozen green beans

Frozen vegetables, e.g. cauliflower, spinach, cabbage

Frozen edamame (100g)

Frozen peas (150g)

Coconut water (400ml)

Almond milk (750ml)

Fresh firm tofu, cooked or raw
(100g)

WEEK 2
Seasonings

Coconut oil

Ground cinnamon

Cumin seeds

Olive oil

Garlic powder

Ground cumin

Barbecue seasoning

Smoked paprika

Nutritional yeast flakes

Tomato purée

Dried oregano

Chilli flakes

Cinnamon sticks

Ground turmeric

Tamari soy sauce

Pomegranate molasses

Ground coriander

Harissa paste

Vegan bouillon powder

White miso paste

Mirin

Rice vinegar

Dijon mustard

Apple cider vinegar

Garlic salt

Flaxseed oil

Chilli powder

Balsamic vinegar

Vanilla and chocolate protein powders

Pantry

Gluten-free oats (215g)

Flaxseed

Ready-to-eat dried apricots (60g)

Chopped tomatoes (3 x 400g tins)

Chickpeas (2 x 400g tins)

Pecan nuts (60g)

Sugar-free vegan chocolate chips (60g)

Desiccated coconut (30g)

Coconut flour (100g)

Coconut milk (1 x 400ml tin)

Mandarin segments in natural juice (1 x 250g tin)

Xylitol (50g)

Dried dates

Quinoa (240g)

Kidney beans (1 x 400g tin)

Vanilla extract

Passata (175g)

Sun-dried tomatoes in oil (1 jar)

Red split lentils (135g)

Almonds (120g)

Walnut pieces (200g)

Mixed seeds

Macadamia nuts (30g)

Chia seeds (80g)

Shelled hemp seeds (30g)

Mixed seeds (100g)

Sunflower seeds (60g)

Pumpkin seeds (60g)

Sesame seeds (100g)

Apple juice (60ml)

Goji berries (60g)

Cocoa powder or raw cacao powder

Almond nut butter

Tahini paste

Fresh fruit and vegetables

Pear (1)

Fresh ginger

Fresh herbs (mint, coriander, basil, parsley)

Broccoli (1 head)

Shiitake mushrooms (250g)

Spinach leaves (300g)

Cauliflowers (3)

Carrots (4)

Mixed salad leaves (4 bags)

Onions (2)

Lemons (3)

Garlic bulbs (2)

Avocado (1)

Red onions (4)

Celery (2 heads)

Romaine lettuces (2)

Red grapes (100g)

Apple (1)

Cucumbers (2)

Spring onions (2 bunches)

Mushrooms (350g)

Red peppers (7)

Tomato (1)

Sweet potato (1)

Aubergine (1)

Courgettes (9)

Grapefruit (1)

Blueberries (140g)

Watercress (1 bag)

Fridge and freezer

Coconut yoghurt (or use homemade)

Unsweetened almond milk (1 litre)

Firm tofu (650g)

Smoked tofu (400g)

Tempeh (400g, or buy additional tofu)

Raw sauerkraut (or use homemade)

Frozen edamame (100g)

Frozen mixed berries (100g)

Frozen broccoli florets

WEEK 3

Seasoning

Sea vegetable mix (1 bag)

White miso paste

Tamari soy sauce

Ground cinnamon

Nutritional yeast flakes

Apple cider vinegar

Rice wine vinegar

Smoked paprika

Ground cumin

Cumin seeds

Chilli powder

Dried oregano

Ground coriander

Mustard seeds

Curry leaves (2)

Tomato purée

Pickled chillies (1 jar)

Capers (1 jar)

Dijon mustard

Red wine vinegar

Garlic salt

Onion salt

Garlic powder

Cayenne pepper

Garam masala

Olive oil

Mirin

Cinnamon sticks

Ground turmeric

Sesame oil

Vegan bouillon powder

Vanilla and chocolate protein powders

Spirulina (optional)

Pantry

Tahini paste

Soft dates (100g)

Chickpea (gram) flour

Ground flaxseed (1 bag)

Whole flaxseed (250g)

Teff flour (200g)

Roasted red peppers (1 jar)

Sun-dried tomatoes in oil (1 jar)

Cocoa powder

Coconut oil

Psyllium husks

Gluten-free oats (290g)

Sugar-free vegan chocolate chips (60g)

Coconut milk (2 x 400ml tins)

Puy lentils (250g)

Chickpeas (1 x 400g tin)

Chia seeds (60g)

Almond nut butter (150g)

Xylitol (1 bag)

Bicarbonate of soda

Baking powder

Vanilla extract

Coconut flour (1 bag)

Quinoa (70g)

Black beans or kidney beans (1 x 400g tin)

Chopped tomatoes (1 x 400g tin)

Butterbeans (3 x 400g tins)

Sunflower seeds (140g)

Pumpkin seeds (15g)

Cashew nuts (40g)

Macadamia nuts (40g)

Sesame seeds (30g)

Red split lentils (250g)

Corn tacos (4)

Black olives in brine (100g)

Probiotic capsules (2, optional)

Fresh fruit and vegetables

Apple (1)

Kale (300g)

Tomatoes (5)

Beansprouts (1 handful)

Mixed salad leaves (4 bags)

Celeriac (250g)

Lemongrass stalk

Fresh herbs (parsley, coriander, thyme, mint)

Green chilli (1)

Red chillies (2)

Limes (4)

Yellow pepper (1)

Avocado (1)

Cauliflower (1 small) or parsnips (2)

Pak choi (3)

Shiitake mushrooms (150g)

Courgettes (5)

Carrots (3)

Celery (1 head)

Fennel bulbs (3)

Onions (4)

Red onions (3)

Red peppers (2)

Cucumber (1)

Garlic bulbs (2)

Spring onions (2 bunches)

Fresh ginger

Cherry tomatoes (550g)

Button mushrooms (300g)

Sugar snap peas (50g)

Mixed salad leaves (2 bags)

Lemons (7)

Bananas (6)

Strawberries (125g)

Kiwi fruit (1)

Pear (1)

Spinach leaves (450g)

Satsuma (1)

Butternut squash (300g)

Green beans (200g)

Fridge and freezer

Coconut yoghurt (350g or use homemade)

Firm tofu (850g)

Apple purée (1 baby food jar)

Almond milk (1 litre)

Kelp noodles (1 bag, optional)

Frozen edamame (200g)

Frozen pitted cherries (125g)

Frozen sweetcorn

Frozen blueberries (30g)

Frozen green vegetables e.g. broccoli

WEEK 4

Seasoning

Olive oil

Smoked paprika

Chilli powder

Chilli flakes

Mustard seeds

Ground coriander

Ground cumin

Cayenne pepper

Ground cinnamon

Ground nutmeg

Garlic powder

Onion salt

Garlic salt

Red hot sauce

Ground turmeric

White miso

Rice wine vinegar

Red wine vinegar

Dijon mustard

Hazelnut or walnut oil

Tamari soy sauce

Coconut oil

Flaxseed oil

Balsamic vinegar

Handful of sea vegetables or
nori sheet

Bag of kelp noodles (optional)

Nutritional yeast flakes

Vegan bouillon powder

Tomato purée

Dried oregano

Matcha green tea powder

Vanilla extract

Vanilla and chocolate protein
powders

Pantry

Tahini

Buckwheat (320g)

Hazelnuts (60g)

Lucuma powder (15g)

Cornflour

Dried mushrooms (15g)

Xanthan gum

Cashew or almond nut butter
(220g)

Cashew nuts (150g)

Acai or goji berry powder
(optional)

Dried berries e.g. cranberries,
cherries (50g)

Desiccated coconut (60g)

Cocoa powder

Almond flour (60g)

Spirulina powder

Chickpea (gram) flour

Quinoa (50g)

Pumpkin seeds (50g)

Gluten-free oats (15g)

Sesame seeds (15g)

Ground flaxseed (70g)

Peanut butter (no added sugar
or salt)

Coconut flour (1 bag)

Chia seeds (50g)

Bicarbonate of soda

Baking powder

Apple purée (1 baby food jar)

Psyllium husks

Xylitol (1 bag)

Mixed seeds (80g)

Pecan nuts (100g)

Cannellini beans (3 x 400g
tins)

Pumpkin purée (1 x 400g tin)

Chickpeas (2 x 400g tins)

Black beans (2 x 400g tins)

Black olives (1 jar)

Roasted red peppers (225g)

Chopped tomatoes (3 x 400g
tins)

Mixed beans (2 x 400g tins)

Kidney beans (2 x 400g tins)

Puy lentils, cooked (500g or
190g dry weight)

Passata (1 carton)

Granulated Stevia

Quinoa (90g)

Coconut milk (150ml)

Red lentils (30g)

Silken UHT tofu (200g)

Fresh fruit and vegetables

Spring onions (2 bunches)

Blueberries (230g)

Watermelon (100g)

Beetroot (4 small)

Baby carrots (300g)

Leeks (2)

Lemons (3)

Garlic bulbs (2)

Carrots (6)

Shiitake mushrooms (300g)

Beansprouts (1 handful)

Fresh herbs (coriander, mint,
parsley, basil)

Chestnut mushrooms (400g)

Mixed mushrooms (450g)

Green beans (300g)

Sweet potatoes (2 medium,
500g total)

Kiwi fruit (1)

Pear (1)

Fresh ginger

Spinach leaves (500g)

Asparagus (125g)

Apples (2)

Cauliflower or broccoli (1
   head, about 400g)

Cauliflower (1 head)

Cucumbers (3)

Red onions (5)

Onions (3)

Red chilli (1)

Radishes (4)

Red peppers (7)

Bananas (6)

Cherry tomatoes (200g)

Tomatoes (12)

Romaine lettuce (1)

Mixed salad leaves (5 bags)

Orange (1)

Courgettes (9)

Avocados (2)

Pomegranates (2)

Aubergines (2)

Red chillies (2)

Portobello mushrooms (8)

Celery (1 head)

Button mushrooms (200g)

Grapefruit (1)

Limes (4)

Watercress or rocket leaves (1
   bag)

Fridge and freezer

Unsweetened almond milk (1
   litre)

Coconut yoghurt (400g or use
   homemade)

Tempeh or tofu (400g)

Firm tofu (700g)

Cooked tofu pieces (400g)

Frozen mixed berries (50g)

Frozen peas (200g)

Bag of frozen vegetables

Index

Acknowledgements

I feel incredibly blessed to be surrounded by such a positive and encouraging family, my inspirational children Nathan, Isaac and Simeon and my loving, supportive husband Chris who are my chief recipe tasters along with numerous clients and fellow nutritional practitioners. Your constant encouragement, support and enthusiasm have been invaluable in everything I do.

I also feel so grateful for the amazing team at Yellow Kite for reaching out to me and encouraging me to create this fabulous book.

Doing what you love is the cornerstone of having abundance in your life, and of discovering lasting health and happiness in seeing others' lives and health transformed. What you choose to put on your fork is more powerful than any pill or medicine to achieve the body you want and the energy and vitality you long for. This book is for anyone looking to make the switch to a plant-based diet and nourish your body from within.

yellow
kite

books to help you live a good life

Join the conversation and tell
us how you live a #goodlife

🐦 @yellowkitebooks
📘 YellowKiteBooks
📌 Yellow Kite Books
📷 YellowKiteBooks